The
ROYAL FAMILY

The
ROYAL FAMILY

A YEAR BY YEAR CHRONICLE OF THE HOUSE OF WINDSOR

Edited by

Duncan Hill • Alison Gauntlett • Sarah Rickayzen • Gareth Thomas

Photographs from the

Daily Mail

Bath • New York • Singapore • Hong Kong • Cologne • Delhi
Melbourne • Amsterdam • Johannesburg • Shenzhen

This edition published by Parragon Books Ltd in 2013 and distributed by

Parragon Inc.
440 Park Avenue South, 13th Floor
New York, NY 10016
www.parragon.com

Produced by Atlantic Publishing

Photographs © Associated Newspapers Archive
except the following © Getty Images on pages: 224br, 225, 226l, 228-9,
234, 235bl, 236t&br, 238t&br, 241t&br, 242 middle &br, 243–255

ISBN: 978-1-4723-3610-1

Printed in China

Contents

Introduction
The House of Windsor

Queen Elizabeth II is only the second monarch in British history to celebrate a Diamond Jubilee. She has been at the center of British life as monarch for 60 years, beginning during the period of postwar austerity and stretching into the second decade of the new millennium.

The House of Windsor was born after George V, mindful of the Royal Family's links with the German monarchy and the negative feelings this could engender, changed the dynastic name from Saxe-Coburg-Gotha to Windsor. Since then, the Royal House has reigned through a period of unprecedented political and social change; the war-weary families of 1918 could not have imagined the Britain of today with its advances in medicine, technology, public health and housing, education, mass communications, political and social attitudes. Then, as the Great War was drawing to a close, Britain still stood at the center of its Empire, and indeed the world, with a Royal Family, distant yet deeply revered by its people. Today, in the second decade of the 21st century, the Empire has long since vanished, and the media and public scrutiny of the Royals has seen an end to the unquestioning loyalties of the past.

The story of the Windsors, especially through the early part of their reign, is a fascinating and at times, dramatic one: George V's death in 1936 led to a constitutional crisis at the end of the year when his eldest son and heir, Edward VIII, abdicated the crown in order to marry Wallis Simpson, an American divorcée. Prince Albert, his second son, was a reluctant king, but he took on the responsibility and the title of King George VI, restoring public confidence in the Royal Family. During World War II, the King and Queen remained at Buckingham Palace or nearby Windsor even during the Blitz, making many morale-boosting visits to the ordinary people of London and the rest of the country.

Sadly, lung cancer caused the early death of the King at the age of 56 in 1952. His elder daughter heard of her father's death while on a tour of Kenya. Having left Britain as a princess, she returned as its Queen and has led the country as its monarch for the past six decades.

These years have not been without their trials and tribulations—the very public separation and divorce of the Prince and Princess of Wales followed by the devastating fire at Windsor Castle led the Queen to describe 1992 as her "annus horribilis"; in 1997, Diana's death in a car crash in Paris brought more grief and sorrow to the Royals, not least the young Princes, William and Harry. These events have, however, been counterbalanced by much happier ones. Many births and marriages have given the family a chance to rejoice. Prince Charles and Princess Anne have remarried and the country recently celebrated the weddings of Prince William to Kate Middleton and Zara Phillips to rugby star Mike Tindall. In 2012, the Queen celebrated the 60th anniversary of her accession to the throne, and she marked the occasion with visits to major cites around Britain and a weekend of celebration in London. This was also the year in which the Olympic Games came to London, with the young Royals playing their part as games ambassadors. In the final month of the year news broke that William and Kate were expecting their first child, the Queen's third great-grandchild.

As Head of State, Queen Elizabeth II has a vital and visible role to play in the life of the nation: an extensive schedule of visits by her and other members of the Royal Family; meeting the public and supporting businesses, charities, and public bodies ensures links with her people are maintained and strengthened. Internationally, her role as Head of the Commonwealth and visits to all parts of the world help to foster and promote positive international relations. Modern communications and "instant" news has meant that many of the members of the Royal Family are recognized the world over; inevitably this has led to increased media interest—some may even say intrusion—and a fascination for all things royal. Being in the public gaze, almost on a daily basis, is something the House of Windsor has had to adapt to, and to accept that they will not always be portrayed in the best of lights. Nevertheless, the Queen and her family are still regarded with great affection and national pride; they have striven to "move with the times" and provide a focus that fosters stability and continuity for the nation.

This book brings together more than 600 photographs from the archives of the *Daily Mail*. Many of them date back to the early years of the 20th century—pictures of George V on the battlefields during the Great War, the young Elizabeth, Duchess of York, on her wedding day—and provide a fascinating and, at times, intimate glimpse of a bygone age. These historic and beautiful pictures are combined, for the first time, with more recent photographs; together, these stunning images catalog the life of the remarkable House of Windsor.

The Young Royals

Edward and Albert were the eldest of six children born to George and Queen Mary. As the firstborn, Edward was the natural heir to the throne.

Right: Edward and his younger sister, Princess Mary, playing with Caesar, the late King Edward's favorite dog, at Frogmore.

Below right: A somewhat awkward and unacademic youth, Edward's younger brother Prince Albert led a rather unhappy childhood, no doubt partly on account of the social stigma associated with his left-handedness and stutter. However, he would later excel at sports, particularly tennis, although here he can be seen playing golf.

Below left: Edward shooting at Balmoral in 1911. Meanwhile, his father was hunting tigers while on a state visit to India.

Opposite right: Edward, resplendent in naval uniform, at Buckingham Palace in 1911, shortly after his father's coronation as King George V, and his own investiture as the Prince of Wales.

Opposite above left: Even as a young man Prince Edward was renowned for his attention to detail when it came to being properly dressed for any given occasion.

Opposite below left: Prince John, the youngest of George V and Queen Mary's six children, suffered from epilepsy. He spent his life hidden from public view and died an early death in 1919.

The Great War

Opposite above: The teenage Prince Albert and Prince Edward, with their sister, Mary, at Balmoral just before the outbreak of war. Prince Albert saw action during the conflict at the great naval Battle of Jutland.

Opposite below left: World War I broke out in 1914 and the King set to work rallying the troops. He visited the trenches on five occasions to conduct inspections and present medals for bravery.

Opposite below right: King George met with General Congreve and Sir Henry Rawlinson on a visit to the Western Front. The King was no stranger to uniform; he had enjoyed a career in the Royal Navy and had risen to the rank of commander.

Left: Britain and France were allied during the conflict and here the King and Queen are pictured with their French counterparts, President and Madame Poincaré.

Below right: The King also took the time to visit French villagers whose lives were seriously disrupted by the fighting.

Below left: Prince Albert participated in a shooting party with Lord Pembroke in October 1920. Here the two men are pictured examining their "bag."

Beginning Royal Duties

Below: After the war, the Princes began to assume Royal duties on behalf of the King. Here Prince Albert, who had become the Duke of York, is pictured kicking off a charity soccer game between Tottenham Hotspur and Corinthians at White Hart Lane, London.

Right: Meanwhile, his brother, the Prince of Wales, demonstrated a commitment to academia when he was installed as Chancellor of the University of Wales in 1921.

Albert's Engagement

Right: Elizabeth Bowes-Lyon, the daughter of the Earl and Countess of Strathmore, had caught Prince Albert's attention when they had met as children. He was immediately attracted to her ease with people, strength of character, and commitment to duty.

Below: Albert and Elizabeth posed for a series of photographs to mark the occasion of their engagement on January 14, 1923. Here they are pictured in a relaxed manner.

Opposite below left: Albert, Duke of York, showed continued support for sports by touring Cambridge University's boathouse.

Opposite below right: The Duke's activities were not limited to sporting life. Here he is pictured giving his support to the postwar rejuvenation of the nation by attending the Reparations for the Empire exhibit.

The Wedding of Albert and Elizabeth

Opposite: Elizabeth is thought to have been reluctant to marry into the Royal Family, but Albert was so in love with her that he persevered, eventually winning her over.

Above left: Albert and Elizabeth were married just three months after their engagement. Elizabeth is pictured leaving her London home on the way to the ceremony.

Above right: The wedding took place at Westminster Abbey on April 26, 1923.

Left: The happy couple are captured on the way to the railroad station to start their honeymoon.

The Honeymoon

Left: The couple spent their honeymoon at Polesden Lacey in Surrey. Here they are seen taking a walk through the grounds. Once the honeymoon was over, they spent the first few years of their marriage living on Bruton Street, London.

Below left: Upon marrying Albert, Elizabeth became the Duchess of York. Here the Duke and Duchess relax after a game of golf.

Below right: The Duke and Duchess pictured with Queen Mary at Balmoral, Scotland, in 1924.

The British Empire Exhibition

Left: The Duke and Duchess of York visited the Millwall Docks in London to talk with workers. After World War I Albert became President of the Industrial Welfare Society and was involved in establishing programs to help young workers.

Below left: In April 1924, the King opened the British Empire Exhibition at Wembley, London, to bolster economic and cultural ties within the Empire. The King returned in May with the Royal Family to attend the Empire Thanksgiving Service.

Below right: The Royal Family visited the exhibition on several occasions; here Queen Mary arrives with her son, Prince George.

The King Visits France

Opposite above: King George V paid tribute at the Tomb of the Unknown Soldier at the Arc de Triomphe in Paris in 1925. He left a wreath bearing the inscription "From George V, to the unknown soldier."

Opposite below left: The Duke of York took part in the celebrations to mark the centennial of Norwich Museum in October 1925.

Opposite below right: The King and Queen in the Great Hall of Bristol University, where they opened new buildings in June 1925.

Above: The Duke of York with dignitaries, including the Lord Mayor, while on a visit to Leeds in 1925. Despite numerous public appearances, the Duke often struggled with public speaking on account of a severe stutter.

Left: The King and Queen pictured with the War Minister Stephen Walsh. Walsh was a member of the Labour Government, which had been elected for the first time ever in 1924.

The Birth of Princess Elizabeth

Above left: Princess Elizabeth was born on April 21, 1926. Here she is pictured on a drive from Buckingham Palace in 1927, accompanied by her nanny, Clara "Allah" Knight.

Above right: Young Princess Elizabeth, at the age of two, leaving her London home for a drive with her nanny.

Far left: The Duke and Duchess were presented with a teddy bear by a well-wisher on a trip to the movies shortly after the birth of their first daughter.

Left: The Duchess of York spent a day watching horse racing at Cheltenham.

Opposite: The Duke of York with his father, the King, at Balmoral, having welcomed King Boris of Bulgaria for a brief visit.

Playing Tennis at Wimbledon

Below: The Duke of York was a keen sportsman and a good tennis player. Here he is seen playing in the Men's Doubles Championship at Wimbledon in 1926. He was the first member of the Royal Family to participate in the tournament.

Right: The King and Queen pictured on their way to Ascot to enjoy a day at the races.

Below right: The Duchess of York watching horse racing at Cheltenham.

A Visit to Australia

Left: From January to June 1927, the Duke and Duchess of York embarked on a tour of Australia and New Zealand. Here a procession of cars carried the Duke and Duchess to Sydney Town Hall for the public reception of the Royal tourists. Their arrival in the city attracted a crowd of over one million people.

Below left: On the long journey the couple passed the time by playing tennis quoits on the deck of HMS *Renown*.

Below right: While in New Zealand, the Duchess of York went fishing for trout at Tokaanu, Lake Wanaka, on the South Island in June 1927.

A Busy Schedule

Above left: The Duke and Duchess of York are photographed leaving a function in Bethnal Green, London, in November 1929.

Above: In October, the Duke took part in the Quorn Hunt at Wymeswold, Leicestershire, with the socialite the Maharanee of Cooch Behar.

Middle: The following February, the Duke and Duchess attended the Salvation Army Composers' Festival at the Congress Hall, Linscott Road, east London.

Bottom: The Duke takes part in the celebrations in Glasgow, where the Duchess was given the Freedom of the City in September 1927.

Opposite above: The Duke and Duchess of York were in attendance at the Braemar Games in September 1929.

Opposite below right: The Duke of York is pictured in his kilt after leaving a sitting of the Assembly of the Church of Scotland in Edinburgh in October 1929.

Opposite below left: The Duke pictured during a visit to Fort William, Scotland, the following year.

Promoting Health and Education

Right: The Duke of York declared the opening of new sports fields at Hampton Wick, London, in May 1930.

Below left: The Duke pictured on the train traveling to Wembley to address 10,000 children from schools across London.

Below right: The Duchess of York was introduced to a newborn baby when she opened a new wing at the North Hertfordshire and South Bedfordshire Hospital in Hitchin in July 1929.

Opposite above: In 1931, the Duke and Duchess of York took a trip to Paris. Here they are pictured leaving the Elysée Palace, following a luncheon with the French President.

Opposite middle: The Duke and Duchess also visited the Town Hall in Paris, where a civic reception was held in their honor. They were photographed with the President of the Municipal Council and the British Ambassador.

Opposite below: The Duchess of York and Queen Mary were seen together at the Royal Opera House, London, in June 1933. They were accompanied by the Duke of York.

The Princesses Begin Their Duties

Opposite above: The Duchess of York is pictured with Princess Elizabeth and Princess Margaret in 1934.

Opposite below left: The Duchess took her two daughters to meet soldiers who had suffered injuries during World War I.

Opposite below right: Princess Elizabeth leaving Westminster Abbey with her grandparents, King George and Queen Mary.

Right: Princess Margaret and Princess Elizabeth, with their parents, meeting members of the Royal Company of Archers.

Below left: The young Princesses attend a tree-planting ceremony at Windsor Great Park.

Below right: The Queen, Princess Mary, the Duchess of York, and Princess Elizabeth on their way to watch the Trooping the Color parade (a military ceremony held each June to mark the "official" birthday of the sovereign) at Horse Guards Parade.

Southampton

Above right: In July 1932, the Duke and Duchess of York attended the Royal Show in Southampton. Here Elizabeth is being introduced to members of the council.

Below left: The Duchess of York returned to the city in 1933 with the King and Queen to open the world's largest dry dock.

Above left: The Royal couple also opened a new civic center, where a group of Girl Guides (Scouts) and Boy Scouts had formed a guard of honor.

Taking Part

Above left: The Duke pictured playing golf in the rain at Roehampton. To avoid getting wet, he wore waterproofs over his clothes.

Above middle: The Duchess of York helped to dig a potato plot on a visit to Sheffield to inspect the mines in July 1934.

Below left: After an illness, the Duke was unable to make a visit to the annual boys' camp he ran at Southwold in Suffolk. Instead he addressed the boys and their supervisors at Buckingham Palace before they set off.

Above right: The Duke was able to attend the next camp. He watched and also participated in many of the sports at the camp and is seen here playing soccer.

The Duke of Kent's Wedding

Above left: In 1934, the King's fourth son, Prince George, became Duke of Kent. In the same year he married Princess Marina of Greece. This photograph was taken when the Duke took his fiancée and her parents to meet his own parents at Balmoral.

Middle left: The Duke and Duchess of York boarding an airliner at Hendon as they prepared to visit the International Exhibition in Brussels. While this was to be the Duchess's first flight, the Duke had previously become the first Royal to obtain a pilot's license.

Below left: In May 1934, the Duke of York attended the British Legion Service and inspected the standards on Horse Guards Parade.

Below: Wearing the uniform of the Irish Guards, the King took part in the Trooping the Color ceremony at Horse Guards Parade on the occasion of his 70th birthday in June 1935.

Royal Duties Begin

Right: Once married, the new Duchess of Kent began her royal duties. Here she is pictured with her husband and the Duke and Duchess of York leaving St. Paul's Cathedral, after the King George V Silver Jubilee celebration service, the year after their wedding.

Below left: Prince Edward, the first son of the Duke and Duchess of Kent, was born in October 1935.

Below right: Princess Elizabeth with the corgi dog Dookie and Princess Margaret with Janie at the Royal Lodge at Windsor.

King George's Silver Jubilee

Right: Crowds lined the Victoria Embankment, London, in 1935 to catch a glimpse of the King and Queen as they returned from the Jubilee celebration service at St. Paul's, which commemorated the 25th anniversary of the King's accession to the throne.

Below left: King George greets one of his admirals aboard the Royal Yacht in 1935.

Below right: During the Temple Bar Ceremony, the Lord Mayor of London presented the King with the ceremonial sword that is the symbol of the City of London's independence.

Opposite: The official Jubilee Portrait of the King and Queen.

The Death of King George V

Below: King George V died on January 20, 1936, at Sandringham House. His body was taken by train to London for the funeral and then transported from King's Cross Station to the Great Hall at the Palace of Westminster.

Left: Long lines formed at Windsor Castle, where wreaths and flowers covered the lawn on the south side of the chapel and rested along the length of the wall on the north side.

Opposite: The closing hours of the lying-in-state of George V before the funeral on January 28.

The Abdication Crisis

Above left: The day after the King's death, the Prince of Wales was proclaimed King Edward VIII. Here he is pictured with his brothers, the Duke of Kent, the Duke of York, and the Duke of Gloucester, at the time of his accession to the throne.

Above right: King Edward VIII delivered his first radio broadcast to his subjects from Broadcasting House in March 1936.

Opposite above left and right: Within months of Edward's accession to the throne, scandal erupted when the King's relationship with a married woman (Mrs. Wallis Simpson) became common knowledge, and pressure mounted for him to abdicate. In December 1936, Edward relented and made his abdication speech from Windsor Castle.

Opposite below left and right: Edward and Wallis Simpson on their wedding day at the Château de Candé in France. The marriage took place six months after the abdication.

Left: After abdicating the throne, Edward became the Duke of Windsor and, as his wife, Wallis became the Duchess. The pair made their home in France and spent much of their time there until his death in 1972 and hers in 1986.

The Coronation of George VI

Opposite above left: After Edward abdicated, his brother Prince Albert acceded to the throne and became King George VI. His coronation took place on May 12, 1937. Here the King and the Queen are pictured leaving for Westminster Abbey in the state coach.

Opposite above right: The King was closely followed by his brothers, the Duke of Gloucester and Duke of Kent, riding on horseback.

Opposite below left: After passing under Admiralty Arch, the procession pressed on toward the Abbey. Here it is pictured on Northumberland Avenue.

Opposite below right: A long procession followed the King's coach. The next to pass through Admiralty Arch were the Yeomen of the Guard, or Beefeaters. They were followed by the Watermen.

Above right: After traveling down The Mall, the King's carriage passed under Admiralty Arch.

Middle right: Parties were held across the country during Coronation week. This picture shows a children's party in Old Pye Street, London.

Below right: Streets were also decorated for the occasion. In this picture Vine Street, London, is festooned with flags.

Following pages: Once in the Abbey, the King swore an oath and received communion.

Taking to the New Job

Below: After the turbulence of the abdication crisis and the euphoria of the Coronation, the new King and Queen began to restore a sense of normality to the monarchy. Here the Queen and Princess Elizabeth and Princess Margaret, dressed in kilts, attend a bazaar at Crathie Church in September 1938.

Bottom left: In March 1938, the King and Queen toured a series of housing projects in London. Here they are pictured chatting to a woman with laundry on the line at Armoury House.

Right: The King affectionately inspects his daughters, dressed in their Girl Guides (Girl Scouts) outfits. One thousand Girl Guides had been invited to Windsor Castle and the occasion marked the first official appearance of the girls in uniform.

Below right: The Queen and her daughters reviewed the Christmas displays on a tour of the toy departments of London's big stores.

Supporting the Arts and Sports

Left: The King inspects and presents colors to the Grenadier Guards in 1939.

Below: The King presented the Football Association Cup to Jimmie Guthrie of Portsmouth Football Club following his team's 4–1 victory over Wolverhampton Wanderers in the final. During the following season the war interrupted the tournament and the final would not to be played again until 1946.

Bottom: Princess Elizabeth accompanied her parents to the All-Star Coliseum Show in 1939.

Entertaining the French President

Left: The King and Queen entertained the French President LeBrun and his wife at the Royal Opera House in London in March 1939. Here the Queen hands her fur wrap to an officer as she arrives.

Above: President and Madame LeBrun, the King and Queen, Queen Mary, and other members of the Royal Family stand for the playing of the French and British national anthems before the gala performance by the Vic-Wells Ballet.

Trip to Canada

Left: The King and Queen leave the Palace to begin their trip to Canada in May 1939.

Below left: Standing on deck during their outbound voyage to Canada.

Below right: The King and Queen tried to see as much of Canada as possible and traveled from coast to coast. Here they are pictured in the Rocky Mountains, on the lower slopes of Mount Robson, where the locals assembled to cheer them.

In the United States

Left: While visiting Canada, the Royal party took a detour to the United States in June 1939. Here their cavalcade passes the Capitol Building while taking the King and Queen to meet President Roosevelt at the White House.

Below left: The Royal Family's ship back from North America heads toward Southampton with an escort from the Royal Air Force.

Below right: The return of the King and Queen is celebrated as they move through the streets of London with Princess Elizabeth and Princess Margaret.

The King Prepares for War

Below right: Just over 20 years after peace was agreed between Britain and Germany, the two nations once again found themselves at war. The King and Queen are pictured on September 3, 1939, following his broadcast to the nation announcing the outbreak of war.

Left: The King also had responsibilities for the Canadian Army. Here he is pictured with Major General Andrew McNaughton, the head of his Canadian forces, in April 1940.

Below left: In order to remain informed of the latest military technology, the King tried out a Bren gun during an inspection of a small-arms factory in June 1940.

Braving the Blitz

Above left: Amid the debris from a bombed London hospital, the Queen paid tribute to the hospital workers, some of whom had been bombed out of their homes and yet continued to work long shifts in the wards.

Middle left: King George VI inspected bomb damage in Bristol in December 1940. Earlier in the month the city had been hit by two major attacks.

Below left: The King met nurses from the Bristol Children's Hospital, which had been hit during an air raid.

Below right: The King and the Queen toured the damage in Salford, Lancashire.

Buckingham Palace Bombed

Above left: Buckingham Palace was bombed on the night of September 13, 1940, and the chapel building was destroyed.

Middle left: Accompanied by her husband and Prime Minister Winston Churchill, the Queen spoke to workers who were helping to clean up after the bombing.

Below left: The King and Queen toured the devastation at the Palace. As a gesture of solidarity with the people of London, the King and Queen continued to reside at Buckingham Palace during the war.

Below right: The bombing of Buckingham Palace was part of the wider London Blitz that caused severe damage and loss of life across the city. The Queen visited the East End of London and chatted with those who had been affected.

Princesses at War

Left: Princess Elizabeth and Princess Margaret helped the war effort by gathering the harvest at Sandringham. Here they are pictured talking to one of the young farmworkers.

Middle left: Suggestions had been made that Princess Elizabeth and Princess Margaret be sent abroad to Canada, where it was safer; but the King and Queen did not want to split the family and believed the girls should share in the wartime experience of the nation. They were evacuated to their wartime home, where they were pictured taking the dog for an outing in July 1940.

Below left: In 1940, at just 14 years of age, Elizabeth made her first radio broadcast. Her address was aimed at the children of Britain and the Commonwealth, especially those who had been evacuated.

Below right: The Queen addressed the nation in November 1939 to reassure the mothers of evacuated children.

A Supporting Role

Above left: In August 1941, the Duke of Kent was in Canada to inspect the Canadian Air Force at the Jackson Building in Ottawa. After the inspection he was photographed with his uncle, the Governor-General, on the lawn at Rideau Hall.

Middle left: On a visit to Calne in Wiltshire, Queen Mary met with a group of workers from the YMCA.

Below left: She also visited the YMCA in Cheltenham, where she paused for a cup of tea and shared a joke.

Above: In September 1941, after conducting a number of inspections, the King and Queen took a break at Balmoral. While there, they attended a service at Crathie Church in honor of National Prayer Day.

The Duke of Kent Inspects

Left: The Duke of Kent examined the devastation caused by fire resulting from heavy bombing in January 1941.

Below right: On the same tour of the devastation in London, the Duke talked with a sergeant who was helping with the clean up.

Bottom right: On a visit to Scotland at the end of January 1941, the Duke of Kent paid a visit of inspection to the Queen's Own Royal West Kent Regiment, of which he was Colonel-in-Chief. Dressed in Air Force uniform, he is pictured inspecting a battalion Guard of Honor.

Below left: Princess Elizabeth accompanied her parents on an inspection of the Household Cavalry at barracks in southern England in December 1940.

The Death of the Duke of Kent

Above: On August 25, 1942, the Duke of Kent was killed in a plane crash. Here his body is carried by Royal Air Force servicemen to an ambulance, which transported the coffin to the Albert Memorial Chapel at Windsor Castle, where the body lay until the funeral.

Left: The Duke's funeral was held on August 30, 1942. Here the Chief Constable of Buckinghamshire offers his sympathies to the Duchess of Kent after leaving the memorial ceremony.

Visiting Dignitaries

Above: On October 24 1942, the Kings of Norway and Yugoslavia took the salute with the British Royal Family.

Middle: During the war, a number of dignitaries from Allied and friendly governments visited the King and Queen. Here Eleanor Roosevelt is pictured during her stay with the Royal Family.

Bottom: In April 1942, Elizabeth celebrated her 16th birthday by making her first appearance in public at an official ceremony. As Colonel-in-Chief, she reviewed the Grenadier Guards at a special birthday parade of her regiment at Windsor Castle.

The Princesses Pitch In

Above left: Elizabeth and Margaret purchased the first two Savings Certificates of the new £1 issue at the Post Office in January 1943.

Above right: Elizabeth (left), as the patrol leader of the Buckingham Palace Girl Guides (Girl Scouts), writes a message for Chief Guide Lady Baden-Powell at Guide Headquarters on the occasion of "Thinking Day" in 1943.

Far left: The message was sent to Lady Baden-Powell by pigeon post. Here Elizabeth carefully attaches the letter to the pigeon.

Left: Elizabeth (right) and Margaret follow the bird as it flies off into the distance toward Guide Headquarters.

Meeting the Forces

Left: In a sign of international solidarity, the King inspected a detachment of the Greek Navy at Chatham in Kent.

Middle: The King was introduced to some airmen in June 1942.

Below: When leaving a service at St. Paul's, the Royal Family were preceded by the Sword of State.

Opposite: Earlier in the year the King had watched England and Wales play a friendly soccer match at Wembley Stadium. Here he is pictured meeting Brian Jones of Wales.

Princess Elizabeth Turns 18

Above: Princess Elizabeth with her parents on her 18th birthday in April 1944.

Left: The Royal Family gathered to celebrate her birthday with a family luncheon hosted by the King and Queen.

The King's Speeches

Above: The King was determined to conquer his stutter and with the help of Lionel Logue, an Australian speech therapist, he was able to overcome most of his difficulties. His Christmas Day broadcast to the nation in 1944 was especially poignant, with so many troops fighting abroad and with so many having lost their lives in the war.

Below: The King is kept informed of the latest progress of the invasion force at a naval base in southern England in November 1944 by the Chief of Staff, Commodore G. Bellars.

Middle: The King and Queen went to Euston Station to see the Duke and Duchess of Gloucester off on their voyage to Australia, where he was to become Governor-General.

Wartime Family Life

Left: The Queen, Queen Mary, and the Duchess of Gloucester are pictured after the christening of Prince Richard, the second son of the Duke and Duchess.

Below left: Despite the war, family life continued for the Royals. Here the Princesses arrive at Westminster Abbey for the marriage of Lady Anne Spencer in February 1944.

Below and bottom right: Sea Ranger Princess Elizabeth shared the chores before setting off in a rowboat in July 1944.

Anglo-American Relations

Left: In October 1944, the King made a visit to France to inspect troops.

Below right: On the trip the King was introduced to the Allied supreme commander, General Eisenhower.

Below left: After the war was over, the King met with President Truman aboard HMS *Renown* in Plymouth Sound. The meeting took place very close to the Mayflower Steps, from where the Pilgrim Fathers set sail for New England in 1620.

War is Over

Above: A famous image of the Royal Family and the Prime Minister Winston Churchill acknowledging the crowds from the balcony at Buckingham Palace on May 8, 1945, Victory in Europe Day.

Left: In May 1945, soon after the end of the war, the King and Queen made another visit to the East End of London. Here they are pictured on Vallance Road in Stepney.

Honoring the War Effort

Left: George VI presented soldiers with the King's Medal at the Mansion House in October 1945. Here the King awards a medal to Kenneth Wood.

Below: The King and Queen met wounded soldiers across the country after the war; here they talk to a group of men in Preston.

Victory in Japan

Above: The King celebrated victory over Japan on the grounds of Buckingham Palace after the State Opening of Parliament. He met politicians and generals, including the new Prime Minister, Clement Attlee (third from left).

Middle: The King and Queen toured Swansea in November 1945 and were welcomed by the Mayor at the Civic Centre, after a visit to an oil refinery at Llandarcy.

Below: The King visited soldiers who had recently been released from German prison camps and were resting in Norfolk, awaiting transport back to India.

Events at Windsor

Above left: Princess Elizabeth planted a red oak in Windsor Great Park to commemorate the work done for the Red Cross by the British Agriculture and Allied interests.

Left: In May 1945, Princess Elizabeth and Princess Margaret won a silver cup at the Royal Windsor Horse Show.

Above right: Princess Elizabeth leaves the clubhouse of the Association of Girls Clubs and Mixed Clubs in London.

Getting Back to Normal

Top left: The King and Queen took particular interest in a young woodworker on a tour of Slough Social Centre in December 1947.

Top right: On the same tour of Slough Social Centre, the King and Queen played a game of darts. The Queen beat the King by two points after three throws.

Above: The King and Queen gave their support to the rejuvenation of British industry by visiting the "Britain Can Make it" Exhibition in September 1946. They are pictured with a leather traveling case, one of many consumer goods that the exhibition sought to showcase.

Right: The Queen and Queen Mary admire an exhibit at the Regency Exhibition at the Brighton Pavilion in July 1946.

South Africa

Top left: The Royal Family headed for South Africa in January 1947. Here they are pictured arriving at Waterloo Station before departure.

Top right: They had a busy schedule, but managed to get away for a short break in the Natal National Park.

Above: Princess Elizabeth turned 21 while the Royal Family was in South Africa. She broadcasted a speech from Cape Town to mark the occasion.

Right: The Royal Family were away for several months and did not return until May 1947. A large crowd gathered at Buckingham Palace to welcome them home. The Royals can be seen on the Palace balcony.

Princess Elizabeth Weds

Opposite: In November 1947, at the age of 21, Princess Elizabeth (pictured here arriving for the ceremony) was married to Philip, who became Duke of Edinburgh after the wedding.

Above: The wedding party was photographed at Buckingham Palace after the ceremony at Westminster Abbey.

Left: The newlyweds greeted the crowds of well-wishers from the balcony at Buckingham Palace.

Overleaf: The crowned heads of Europe joined members of the Royal Family to celebrate the wedding.

Silver Wedding Anniversary

Above: April 1948 marked the 25th wedding anniversary of the King and Queen. The family celebrated with a visit to St. Paul's Cathedral. After the service they appeared on the balcony at Buckingham Palace (opposite above) to wave to the large crowd that had amassed outside.

Opposite below: The following month, the King and Queen visited the British Industries Fair at Earls Court, London, with Harold Wilson, the President of the Board of Trade. They attended the heavy industries section of the fair in Birmingham a few days later.

Scotland

Left: The Royal Family were in Scotland in July 1948, where they visited the Northern Infirmary in Inverness.

Below left: On the same tour, the Royal party watched a parade of ponies with the Minister of Agriculture, Tom Williams.

Below: During his trip to Scotland, the King drove from Edinburgh to attend the Open Golf Championship at Muirfield.

London Olympics

Top: In August 1948, London hosted the first postwar Olympics. The King and Queen watched athletics at Wembley on the Queen's 48th birthday.

Above: The King, Queen, and other spectators stand for the anthem at the London Olympics.

Left: The King pauses for a cigarette during play at Muirfield.

The Birth of Prince Charles

Above: On November 14, 1948, Princess Elizabeth gave birth to her first son, Charles Philip Arthur George. Before the announcement was made, excited crowds gathered outside Buckingham Palace.

Left: The young Prince out for a stroll with his nanny in October 1949.

Opposite above: The King, the Queen, Princess Elizabeth, and Princess Margaret settle into the Royal Box for an evening at the London Coliseum.

Opposite below right: The Queen pictured at a gala ballet performance at the Royal Opera House in honor of the visit of President and Madame Auriol of France in March 1950.

Opposite below left: The Queen is seen talking to Gloria Swanson at the Royal Film Performance of *The Mudlark* at the Empire Theatre in Leicester Square.

Watching Soccer

Above left: George VI was in the stands to watch the 1950 Cup Final between Arsenal and Liverpool at Wembley. Here the King is being introduced to Denis Compton of Arsenal.

Below left: The King and Queen arriving at the Army Cup Final held at Aldershot in March 1950.

Above right: The Royal couple visited the Master Mariners Company ship on the Thames Embankment at Temple Steps in 1950.

Below right: In May 1950, the King and Queen toured the Chelsea Flower Show at the Royal Hospital in Chelsea, London.

Festival of Britain

Above left: The Royal Family visited the South Bank site of the Festival of Britain in May 1951. The South Bank of the Thames River had been completely regenerated as part of the Festival.

Above right: Even the 84-year-old Queen Mary visited the exhibition with her two grandsons, Prince William of Gloucester and Prince Michael of Kent.

Left: The King is pictured signing the visitors' book at the Festival of Britain site.

Above: The Royal Family at Ascot races in 1951.

Balmoral

Top right: In August 1951, the Royal Family arrived at Ballater Station to start their vacation at Balmoral.

Top left: Ballater Station: The Queen with Prince Charles and Princess Anne, who was born on November 15, 1950.

Above: The following week the King and Queen were invited to dinner at the Danish Embassy by the Danish monarchs.

Right: The Queen and Princess Margaret during an inspection of an Australian ship.

The Young Princes

Left: Prince Charles and Prince Richard of Gloucester were taken for a stroll through Green Park, London, in November 1951.

Below left: While being taken for a walk, Prince Charles shows an interest in one of the soldiers on duty at Clarence House in August 1951.

Below right: Prince Charles enjoyed his first visit to an airport at two and a half years old, when he went to greet his mother on her return from Malta. He is seen holding the Princess's hand after she had disembarked from the airplane.

The King's Last Trip to Balmoral

Top: The King and Queen returned to the Braemar Highland Games in September 1951 with Princess Margaret.

Above left: Lord Lovat guided the King and Queen around the highland show.

Above right: George Clark was presented to the King and Queen after "tossing the caber" at the Braemar Games.

Right: The King returned from Scotland ahead of the rest of the Royal Family after his medical advisers suggested he have a thorough medical checkup. He is pictured here in the car traveling between Euston railroad station and Buckingham Palace.

The Death of King George VI

Above: The *Daily Mail's* last photograph of the King was taken at London Airport, where he had been saying good-bye to Princess Elizabeth as she departed on a tour of the Commonwealth.

Above right: The King died on February 6, 1952. This is how the event was covered by the London *Evening Standard*.

Below left: The neon lights at the normally vibrant Piccadilly Circus were turned off as a mark of respect.

Below right: Floral tributes amassed on the grounds of Windsor Castle.

THE KING DIES IN HIS SLEEP

A peaceful end this morning

The Evening Standard announces with deep regret that the King died early this morning.

The announcement came from Sandringham at 10.45 a.m. It said: "The King, who retired to rest last night in his usual health, passed peacefully away in his sleep early this morning."

With him at Sandringham were the Queen, Princess Margaret and the King's grandchildren, Prince Charles and Princess Anne.

The King was 56. It is 136 days since the operation on his lung. Yesterday he was out rabbit shooting for several hours. To everybody he appeared to be in the very best of health.

To-day he had planned to go out shooting hares. But when gamekeepers went to Sandringham House for instructions they were told: "The shoot is cancelled."

One doctor was called to Sandringham before the announcement of the King's death was made. He was 37-year-old Dr. James Ansell, local man who held the title of Surgeon Apothecary to the Sandringham Household.

News of her father's death was telephoned to Princess Elizabeth, the new Sovereign, in Africa. She decided to fly home immediately.

She is due to arrive at 4.30 p.m. to-morrow and will meet the Privy Council to give orders for Court mourning and the funeral.

By then she will have been proclaimed Queen—at an Accession Council at St. James's Palace at five o'clock this evening.

The story of the King's last shoot was told this afternoon by one of his party, Lord Fermoy. He said: "Yesterday was one of the loveliest winter days I have ever known in Norfolk.

"It was perfect for shooting and the King was ready to move off soon after 9.30.

"He was in great form. He was a...

This is the picture that first told the people of Britain that all was not well with the King. It was taken on May 3 last year when the King was driving back to Buckingham Palace after the Festival of Britain dedication service at...

The new Queen flies home to-night

From EVELYN IRONS : Nyeri, Wednesday

Princess Elizabeth heard the news of her father's death 45 minutes after the announcement from Sandringham.

She was told by Prince Philip. A member of her household said: "She stood it very bravely, like a Queen."

Arrangements were made immediately for the Princess and the Prince to fly home to-night.

The news was telephoned to the Royal Lodge by a Nairobi newspaper.

It was decided to withhold it until direct confirmation was obtained from Buckingham Palace.

Palace call

Soon afterwards a direct radio-telephone call came through from the Royal Family.

The call was routed to the Princess through a little country post offices in the Kenya countryside.

It took nearly 30 minutes for the call to be properly connected and established from London.

Then the Princess and the Prince left the Royal Lodge here by car and drove to the airfield at Nanyuki where a Dakota of East African Airways waited to fly them to Entebbe, Uganda.

6.30 p.m. take-off

They were taking off at 6.30 p.m. from Entebbe, Uganda, for home in the

● Page Two, Col. Four

LYING IN STATE NEXT WEEK

At Westminster Hall

The body of the King will be taken to Westminster Hall, probably this week-end.

It will lie in state on a catafalque in the centre of the hall throughout, next week beginning on Monday.

A guard will be maintained night and day.

The funeral is expected to take place early in the following week.

Parliament will be adjourned until after the funeral—probably for ten days or a fortnight.

ONE PROGRAMME ON BBC AND ALL SHOWS CLOSE

Shops clear gay windows

The announcement of the King's death was made on the BBC at 11.15 a.m. Announcer John Snagge added: "The BBC offers profound sympathy to her Majesty the Queen and the Royal Family."

Then the BBC closed down for the rest of the day except for news, special bulletins, shipping forecasts and gale warnings.

A short service will be broadcast at 9.15 to-night.

The Home and Light programmes are to merge until after the funeral. To-morrow serious music will be broadcast on all stations.

On Friday some other suitable programmes may be broadcast. The Third Programme was broadcast independently before the funeral, but a single programme will be sent out for the next two days.

The overseas broadcasts will give serious music for the next 24 hours with news and special bulletins. Programmes go back to normal after the funeral.

The television service announced the news then closed on the demonstration film at 11.30 a.m.

At 11.45 screens showed the BBC coat of arms with the

▲ Page Two, Col. Five

WEATHER—Cloudy

Lying in State

Above: The King's body lying in state in Westminster Hall. Four gold candelabra from Westminster Abbey stand at the four corners of the coffin, which was guarded continuously by officers of the Household Troops—members of the King's Bodyguard and the King's Gentlemen at Arms. The body remained in the Hall for three days, allowing members of the public to file past the coffin.

Middle: On the day of his death, the Honourable Artillery Company fired one shot per minute for each of the 56 years of the King's life. A similar salute was given in Hyde Park.

Below: Crowds gathered at Buckingham Palace's gates to pay their respects.

The Funeral of King George VI

Left: People paid their final respects to the King as his coffin proceeded toward his final resting place in St. George's Chapel, Windsor.

Below left: A close-up of the cortege with the coffin as it passed down Horse Guards Parade.

Below right: The first public proclamation of the accession of Queen Elizabeth II is read from the balcony at Friary Court, St. James's Palace, on February 8, 1952.

The Coronation of Queen Elizabeth II

Above left: Elizabeth was officially crowned Queen on June 2, 1953, at Westminster Abbey, with some 8,000 people in attendance, while millions more were able to watch the ceremony on television for the first time. She begins her journey to the Abbey in the gold state coach.

Above right: Wearing a simple white dress, the Queen is seated in St. Edward's Chair, surrounded by Knights of the Garter, as she prepares for the Ceremony of the Anointing.

Right: She bears the Rod with Dove, symbol of equity and mercy, in her left hand, and the Scepter with Cross, the symbol of power and justice, in her right, while the Archbishop of Canterbury prepares to place St. Edward's Crown on her head.

Opposite: Having spoken private prayers, the Queen takes the Chair of Estate.

Following pages: After the formal proceedings, the Queen and her attendants leave Westminster Abbey.

In the evening, the Queen appeared on the balcony of Buckingham Palace to greet the cheering crowds that thronged below and to watch the flyby salute by the Royal Air Force.

Official Birthday

Opposite above: A year after the Coronation, the Queen's "official birthday" was marked with a flyby by the Royal Air Force. Prince Charles and Princess Anne joined Princess Margaret and the Queen Mother to watch from the balcony.

Opposite below: The family again gathered on the balcony later that year as crowds below chanted birthday wishes to the Duke of Edinburgh during the Trooping the Color ceremony.

Above: Swathed in white fur, the Queen attended the Order of the Bath ceremony in Westminster Abbey.

Right: The Queen arrives at Victoria Palace for the annual Royal Variety Show in November 1955.

Passion for Horses

Top and middle right: A chance for the Queen and the Duke of Edinburgh to spend a family day together with Prince Charles and Princess Anne at a polo match in 1956.

Below right: In the same year, the Queen and the Duke made a Royal visit to South Uist and Benbecula in Scotland. The Duke drove to the proposed site of the North Ford bridge.

Below left: A chance for the Queen to spend time playing with Princess Anne and her pony Greensleeves during the family summer vacation in Balmoral.

Opposite above: The Queen Mother took the opportunity to walk to the paddock before the start of the Derby at Epsom races. She was accompanied by the Earl of Rosebery.

Opposite below left: The Queen and Duke of Edinburgh walked in procession to Windsor Castle for the service of the Order of the Garter in St. George's Chapel.

Opposite below right: The Queen and Princess Margaret spoke to jockey Dick Francis at Aintree. He was about to ride the Queen Mother's horse, Devon Loch.

Royal Visit to Guernsey

Opposite above left: During a visit to St. Peter Port in Guernsey, the Queen was presented with a bouquet by Hilary Beacher.

Opposite above right: She also visited Elizabeth College on the island, where 6,000 children sang her a "song of welcome," much to her obvious delight.

Opposite below left: In 1957, the World Scout Jamboree took place in Sutton Park in Warwickshire. The Queen visited the site and is pictured as she passes the arch of the Iranian Scouts, one of the features of the camp.

Opposite below right: The Queen just after she had broadcast her Christmas Day message to the nation in 1957.

Above left: During the summer of 1959, the Queen visited the Royal Botanical Gardens at Kew, which celebrated its bicentennial. She visited the refurbished Palm House and had tea in the Orangery.

Above right: Prince Charles and Princess Anne in December 1957.

Middle left: Children climbed onto the St. Albans Abbey windowsills to watch the Queen and the Duke of Edinburgh leave after a church service.

Below left: Prince Charles on his way to see a gala performance of *The Nutcracker*, given in aid of the Royal Ballet Benevolent Fund at the Royal Opera House, Covent Garden, London.

Formal Occasions

Opposite above: In November 1958, the Queen attended a dinner held at the American Embassy in London hosted by the Vice President Richard Nixon.

Opposite below left: The Queen with Lord Mountbatten at the premiere of *Dunkirk* in 1958.

Opposite below right: Later in the year, she was present at the Odeon, Leicester Square, for the premiere of Danny Kaye's movie *Me and the Colonel*, where guests included Nicole Maurey and Mr. and Mrs. Curt Jurgens.

Left and below right: The Queen and Duke of Edinburgh enjoy the chance to relax on the grounds of Windsor Castle, just prior to setting off for a tour of North America.

Below left: Despite the rain, the Queen and Duke cheerfully greeted the crowds at the Royal Ascot race meeting in 1960.

Princess Margaret Marries

Opposite above left and right: On May 6, 1960, Princess Margaret left Clarence House with the Duke of Edinburgh, who was to give her away. They made the journey to Westminster Abbey, where she was to marry Antony Armstrong-Jones.

Left: The magnificent wedding ceremony at Westminster Abbey was conducted by the Archbishop of Canterbury, Dr. Geoffrey Fisher. The bride was accompanied by her eight bridesmaids and Dr. Roger Gilliat was best man.

Opposite below left: Princess Margaret and Antony Armstrong-Jones enter their coach after the ceremony.

Opposite middle right: They traveled in the Queen's coach, which was cheered by the crowds as it passed down The Mall.

Opposite below right: The thousands lining The Mall surged forward in their enthusiasm to greet the newly married couple.

The Birth of Prince Andrew

Top and above: The newlyweds went out onto the balcony at Buckingham Palace to greet the cheering well-wishers that thronged into The Mall. They were joined by other members of the Royal Family.

Left: Princess Margaret was one of the members of the Royal Family invited to dine with the King and Queen of Siam at the Thai Embassy in London.

Opposite above left: The Queen Mother holds the infant Prince Andrew on her 60th birthday at Clarence House. Prince Charles and Princess Anne were also there to enjoy the celebrations. He was born on February 19, 1960.

Opposite above right: Princess Margaret and Antony Armstrong-Jones left King's Cross Station to take a train to Balmoral in August 1960 amid speculation that she was expecting a baby, which proved to be unfounded.

Opposite below: Precious family time at Balmoral as they all enjoy playing with baby Prince Andrew.

The Duke of Kent Marries

Above: In April 1961, the Duke of Kent was married to Miss Katharine Worsley. He wore the uniform of his regiment, the Royal Scots Guards.

Right: Princess Margaret and her husband, Antony Armstrong-Jones, attended the Duke of Kent's wedding. In October, Armstrong-Jones was to accept the title Earl of Snowdon.

Opposite above left: Prince Charles at the three-day Badminton Horse Trials.

Opposite above right: The Queen spends time with her eldest son at the trials.

Opposite below left: The Queen surveying the scene at Badminton.

Opposite below right: In July, the Queen presented the John Player trophy to Pat Smythe, the winner of the International Horse Showjumping Competition.

Meeting the President

Left: In June 1961, the Queen met the new President of the United States, John F. Kennedy, and his wife, Jackie, at a reception held at Buckingham Palace.

Opposite above left: The family gather for the Trooping the Color ceremony in 1962. A young Prince Andrew waves to the crowds.

Opposite right: The Queen leaves the London Palladium after watching the Royal Variety Show.

Opposite below left: Later in the year, she was present for the premiere of *Lawrence of Arabia* at the Leicester Square Odeon in London.

Grand Occasions

Above left: The Queen presents the championship trophy to Rod Laver, winner of the Men's Singles competition at Wimbledon.

Above right: A chance for mother and daughter to look around at Badminton.

Below left: The Queen at London Airport just before flying to The Netherlands.

Below right: In October 1962, the Queen greeted the stars at the Royal Command Performance held at the London Palladium. She can be seen shaking hands with Cliff Richard, who stands alongside Harry Secombe and Eartha Kitt.

Royal Visits

Above left: The Queen Mother and Viscount Linley, Princess Margaret's son, on their way to Crathie Church near Balmoral.

Above right: The Queen signs the visitors book after a visit to the Naval and Military Club.

Below left: In July 1965, Elizabeth II became the first reigning monarch since 1671 to make an official visit to the Isle of Wight. At Carisbrooke Castle she installed Earl Mountbatten as "Governor and Captain of All Our Isle of Wight."

Below right: The Queen was introduced to the comedian Ken Dodd at the Royal Variety Performance held at the London Palladium. Spike Milligan and Max Bygraves are also pictured.

The Birth of Prince Edward

Opposite above and Above: On the Queen's 39th birthday, she spent time with her family, including Prince Edward, who was born on March 10, 1964, at Frogmore House, which is situated in Home Park, below Windsor Castle.

Opposite below left: The Queen in Belfast, Northern Ireland, in July 1966.

Opposite below right: The Queen accompanies the Marquess of Exeter in the front seat of a Land Rover at the Burghley Horse Trials World Championships.

A Family Reunion

Above: A momentous occasion in the family's history: in 1967, the Queen met the Duke of Windsor for the first time since his abdication 30 years previously. They had joined together to unveil a plaque in memory of Queen Mary, the Duke's mother and the Queen's grandmother. (Left to right: the Queen Mother, the Duke and Duchess of Gloucester, the Duke and Duchess of Windsor, and the Queen.)

Right: The annual Order of the Garter ceremony at Windsor.

Opposite above left: Prince Edward is anxious to board the Royal train as he tugs at the Queen's hand before they head to Balmoral.

Opposite above middle: In September 1966, the Queen visited the British Aircraft Corporation Works in Filton, Bristol, but was late leaving due to her interest in the progress of the Anglo-French Concorde project.

Opposite above right: Prince Charles, Princess Anne, and Prince Philip on their return from Jamaica.

Opposite below left: An elementary school in London received a visit from the Queen in February 1967.

Opposite below right: Princess Anne congratulated Betty Hanaway and her horse Grey Leg. They had just won the Queen Elizabeth II Cup at the Royal International Horse Show at White City, London.

Happy Birthday

Opposite: The Royal Family pictured at Windsor on the Queen's
42nd birthday in 1968.

Above: Prince Charles leaves a church service with the Queen
Mother and other members of the Royal Family.

President Nixon

Above: In February 1969, the Queen and Prince Philip were joined for lunch at Buckingham Palace by President Richard Nixon.

Left: Prince Charles accompanied his parents and sister to the 25th anniversary Variety Performance, held in aid of the Army Benevolent Fund.

Opposite above: Christmas 1969 and the ten Royal grandchildren are photographed together on the East Terrace at Windsor after the morning service in St. George's Chapel. Left to right: Master James Ogilvy; Lady Sarah Armstrong-Jones; the Earl of St. Andrews; Lady Helen Windsor; the Prince of Wales; Viscount Linley; Prince Andrew; Miss Marina Ogilvy; Princess Anne, and Prince Edward.

Opposite middle left: Princess Margaret and Lord Snowdon left London Airport for a week's tour of Yugoslavia. It was the first official visit by a member of the Royal Family to a Communist country.

Opposite below left: Both Prince Charles and Princess Anne attended the gala performance of *The Nutcracker* given in aid of the Royal Ballet Benevolent Fund at the Royal Opera House, Covent Garden.

Opposite below right: A smiling Princess Anne shies away from the cameras at the racecourse.

Out and About

Opposite above left: The Queen, Princess Anne, and Prince Charles seen arriving at the "Talk of the Town" for a Royal Gala Cabaret in aid of the World Wildlife Fund.

Opposite above right: The Queen Mother at the Badminton Horse Trials with her grandchildren Prince Andrew, Viscount Linley, and Lady Sarah Armstrong-Jones.

Opposite below left: The Queen Mother celebrated her 70th birthday at Clarence House with Prince Edward and his young cousins, Lady Sarah and Viscount Linley.

Opposite below right: The family plans a forthcoming trip to Australasia.

Above right: The Queen, Prince Philip, and Prince Edward at the Royal Windsor Horse Show. The pair of grays in the foreground were part of the team entered by the Queen for the three-day driving event.

Right: The Queen and Prince Edward at Badminton in April 1971. The following year Princess Anne became European Champion at the three-day horse trials held at Burghley in September, despite an operation to remove an ovarian cyst the month before.

Below left: The Queen and Princess Anne seen leaving Heathrow Airport for the state visit to New Zealand and Australia.

Time to Relax

Left: The Royal couple at Balmoral.

Below left: The Prince of Wales and the Duke of Edinburgh at Royal Airforce College Cranwell, where the Prince received his "wings" after qualifying as a pilot.

Below right: The Prince of Wales at a charity cricket match during his stay at Cranwell.

Royal Engagement

Above left: Princess Anne and Captain Mark Phillips on the grounds of Buckingham Palace following the announcement of their engagement in May 1973.

Above right: The Queen visited St. Peter's Church of England School in London as part of their centennial celebrations.

Below left: The Queen, Prince Philip, and Prime Minister Edward Heath attended the "Fanfare for Europe" gala at Covent Garden, London.

Below right: The Queen at Balmoral.

Horses and Hounds

Above left: The Queen attended the Royal Windsor Horse Show with King Constantine of Greece and the husband of Princess Margaretha of Sweden, Mr. John Ambler.

Above right: The Queen, Prince Philip, Prince Andrew, and Prince Edward visited the Duke of Beaufort's hounds.

Left: The Queen's bodyguard; Her Majesty inspected the bodyguard of the Yeomen of the Guard at Buckingham Palace.

Princess Anne

Above left: Princess Anne at a showjumping event.

Above right: Princess Anne at Amberley Horse Show with her new pet dog.

Below left: Princess Anne falling from her horse while competing at the European Cross Country Championships in Russia.

Below right: Princess Anne competing in a one-day event at Amberley Horse Show, Cirencester.

Princess Anne Marries

Opposite: After an engagement announcement in May, the Queen's only daughter married Captain Mark Phillips on November 14, 1973, at Westminster Abbey, watched by millions of viewers world-wide. Here the Princess arrives at Westminster Abbey.

Right: The Princess and her husband leaving the Abbey after the service.

Below: After the wedding ceremony the Royal couple greeted well-wishers from the balcony at Buckingham Palace.

Prince Charles Grows into his Public Role

Above left: Both the Prince of Wales and his sister continued to increase their Royal engagements. Here Prince Charles, with the Queen and Princess Alexandra, attends a production of Alan Ayckbourn's play *Absurd Person Singular* at the Vaudeville Theatre.

Above right: The Queen and the Duke of Edinburgh with Prince Edward at Stratfield Saye House, the home of the Duke of Wellington.

Below right: Prince Charles at the British Sub-Aqua Club banquet at the Guildhall.

Duties for a Princess

Above right: Princess Anne taking the salute as Chief Commandant of the Women's Royal Naval Service at a parade at HMS *Dauntless* in Burghfield, Berkshire.

Middle right: The Queen and Princess Margaret at the Royal Windsor Horse Show.

Below right: Princess Anne at the award celebrations of the Society of Film and Television Arts.

Below left: Princess Anne and Captain Mark Phillips at the Amberley Horse Trials.

Kidnap Attempt

Above: While on a state visit to Indonesia in March 1974, the Queen received news that Princess Anne and her husband, Mark Phillips, had thwarted a kidnap attempt while being driven down The Mall in London. Four people received gunshot wounds during the incident, including the Princess's bodyguards and chauffeur. Here policemen are combing the sidewalk for a bullet just feet from the spot where Princess Anne's car was forced to stop during the kidnap attempt.

Left: The shattered windshield of a taxi, caught in the incident in The Mall, stands behind a policeman searching for evidence.

Family Horse ride

Above: The Queen horseback riding with other members of the Royal Family at Ascot. Captain Mark Phillips and Prince Charles are leading the group, followed by the Queen and Princess Anne.

Below right: The Queen Mother on the grounds of Clarence House on her 75th birthday.

Below left: The Queen said thank you to the heroes who helped foil the kidnap attempt by presenting them with gallantry awards.

76th Birthday

Above right: The Queen Mother with her grandchildren (left to right); Viscount Linley, Prince Edward, and Lady Sarah Armstrong-Jones on the grounds of Clarence House on her 76th birthday.

Above left: The Queen at the Badminton Horse Trials with Pipkin the dachshund (who belonged to her sister, Princess Margaret).

Left: The Queen with her sons, Prince Charles, Prince Andrew, and Prince Edward, attend the Montreal Olympic Games to watch her daughter, Princess Anne, compete in the equestrian event.

The Queen's Silver Jubilee

Above: In 1977, the Queen and the country celebrated 25 years of Elizabeth's reign, and the public demonstrated massive support for the monarch. She undertook an extensive tour of both the United Kingdom and the Commonwealth, during which huge crowds lined the streets and gathered outside Buckingham Palace to show their affection.

Left: The official celebrations began at Windsor in June, with the Queen lighting the first of 100 beacons, and with the Royal Family attending a service at St. Paul's Cathedral.

Watching Events

Above left: Prince Charles at the Powys Game Fair.

Above right: The Queen and the Duke of Edinburgh pictured at the Badminton Horse Trials in 1978.

Below right: The Queen is highly amused by an incident at the Badminton Horse Trials.

State Opening of Parliament

Left: Sitting upon the throne, and wearing her reading glasses, the Queen prepares to deliver her speech at the 1978 State Opening of Parliament. She outlined the plans of the government to try to bring inflation and unemployment under control.

Above right: The Queen gives racing advice to Princess Michael of Kent in the Royal Box at Epsom.

Below right: The Queen is pictured clearly enjoying her day out at Epsom races. She was there to see her horse, English Harbour, compete in the Derby.

The Death of Lord Mountbatten

Opposite above left: The news of the assassination of Lord Mountbatten on August 27, 1979, shook the Royal Family. An IRA bomb, which had been planted on his yacht, killed him and three others, including his 14-year-old grandson.

Right and Opposite below: The funeral of Lord Mountbatten took place at Westminster Abbey with the whole Royal Family in attendance.

Opposite above right: Lord Mountbatten was especially close to Prince Charles as a friend and mentor. This picture indicates some of the emotion the Prince was feeling at the funeral.

Saudi Arabia

Opposite above left: The Queen arrived in Riyadh, Saudi Arabia, at the beginning of 1979 for a three-week tour of the Persian Gulf. Upon arriving at the airport she respected the local law and ensured that both her ankles and arms were covered by a long sapphire-blue dress.

Opposite below left: While in Bahrain, the Queen attended a horse race despite the 90-degree heat and the swirling desert winds.

Opposite right: The Queen Mother arriving at the Odeon, Leicester Square, for a screening of *California Suite*. Princess Margaret and Princess Anne joined her for the evening out.

Above and right: The Queen and the Duke of Edinburgh spent time at Balmoral in November 1979 to celebrate their 32nd wedding anniversary. Their four children accompanied them on the visit as well as their young grandson, Peter Phillips.

Lady Diana Spencer

Right: Although they had first met in 1977, it was not until 1980 that a relationship began to blossom between Prince Charles and Lady Diana Spencer, and the media began to take an increasing interest. Diana was no stranger to the Royal Family, her first home having been Park House on the grounds of Sandringham and her childhood playmates included Prince Andrew and Prince Edward.

Below left: When Diana returned home after a visit to Balmoral with the Royal Family, she found the press camped outside her apartment in Coleherne Court, London.

Below right: Diana worked as a kindergarten supervisor, and although not formally trained, demonstrated a natural ability when it came to caring for children.

Opposite: The relationship moved swiftly and, on February 24, 1981, the couple officially announced their engagement.

Preparations

Above left: Diana's engagement ring consisted of a large sapphire set in white gold, surrounded by 14 diamonds.

Left: Diana soon moved in to Buckingham Palace and began to accompany the Prince to official functions and public events. Here she is pictured with Andrew Parker Bowles at the Horse and Hound Grand Military Gold Cup at Sandown, in which Charles was competing.

Top right: While Charles and Diana prepared for their wedding, Princess Anne gave birth to a baby daughter, Zara Phillips, in May 1981.

Above: The Queen Mother is pictured on the balcony at Clarence House, where crowds had gathered to sing "Happy Birthday."

The Wedding of Charles and Diana

Below: Charles and Diana's wedding was a truly spectacular occasion. The service took place at St. Paul's Cathedral, instead of at Westminster Abbey, which was more traditional, and the day was declared a national holiday. A million people were estimated to have lined the processional route from St. Paul's to Buckingham Palace, while some 700 million watched the event on television.

Above left: The newlyweds emerged from the Cathedral to rapturous applause, before proceeding to their waiting coach. Diana's dress had been designed by David and Elizabeth Emanuel and included a 25-foot train.

Above right: Accompanied by a mounted escort, the happy couple were conveyed to Buckingham Palace in their open-top coach, where a huge crowd gathered to greet them.

Honeymooners

Above: A smiling Diana waves to the crowd.

Right: Charles and Diana pictured on their honeymoon at Balmoral, following a brief stay at Broadlands and a two-week cruise around the Mediterranean aboard the Royal Yacht *Britannia*.

Opposite above left: Prince Charles meets Mark Davies, who was injured during the attack on the naval ship *Sir Galahad* during the Falklands War.

Opposite above right: In 1982, the Queen visited the most famous street in Britain when she and Prince Philip inspected the newly built outdoor location for the long-running television program, *Coronation Street*.

Opposite below right: In 1982, the Commonwealth Games were held in Brisbane, Australia. Here the Queen hands the baton to England's Brendan Foster.

Opposite below left: The Queen takes a picture of the closing ceremony of the Commonweath Games in Brisbane.

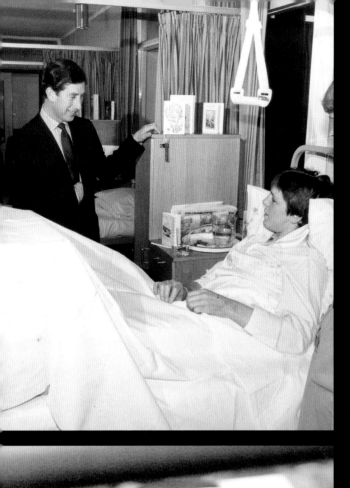

President Reagan

Above: The Queen and the Duke of Edinburgh entertained President and Nancy Reagan at Windsor in 1982.

Left: Princess Anne mimes drinking to her father at Epsom races in 1982.

The Birth of Prince William

Right: On June 21, 1982, Princess Diana gave birth to a son, William Arthur Philip Louis, who became second in line to the throne. He was born at 9:03 P.M. after a 16-hour labor and weighed 7 lb. 1 oz. The Queen ordered a 41-gun salute at Hyde Park and at the Tower of London.

Above: William was christened on August 4 in the Music Room at Buckingham Palace. The Archbishop of Canterbury led the ceremony and the Prince was baptized using water from the Jordan River, a Royal tradition dating back to the time of the Crusades.

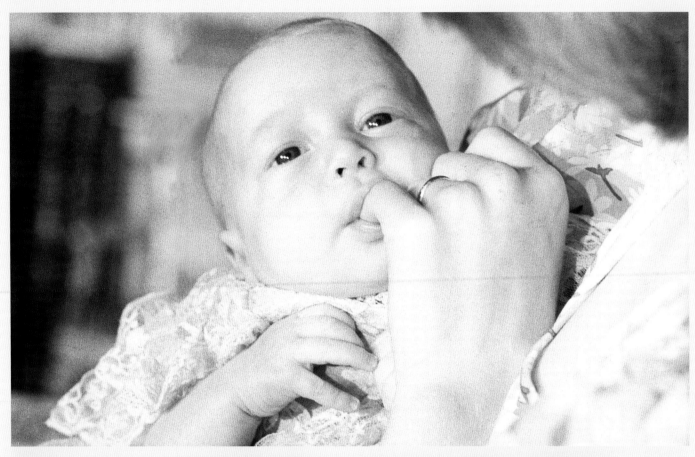

Back to a Busy Schedule

Opposite above: A contented Prince William sucks on his mother's finger.

Opposite below: In November, just months after the birth, Charles and Diana visited Wales, where they are pictured in Aberdovey.

Above right: The Royal Family had lunch at Clarence House to mark the Queen Mother's 83rd birthday in August 1983.

Middle left: In March 1983, the Queen and her grandson Peter Phillips were forced to walk because they could not find their driver after watching Prince Philip in a carriage driving event at the Royal Windsor Horse Show.

Middle right: During another equestrian event in 1984, the Queen took care of her young granddaughter Zara Phillips, while Princess Anne was busy at work.

Bottom right and left: Princess Anne walks the dog with her children while taking a break from the Tetbury Horse Trial in September 1984.

The Birth of Prince Harry

Left and Below left: On September 15, 1984, two years after the arrival of Prince William, Princess Diana gave birth to her second son, Prince Henry Charles Albert David.

Below right: Hordes of photographers and well-wishers waited outside the hospital for the Princess to emerge with her newborn son.

Opposite above: Earlier in the year, the Queen hosted a special banquet for heads of state at Buckingham Palace, following the London Economic Summit. Margaret Thatcher and Ronald Reagan were among the guests.

Opposite below left and right: The Queen and Prince Philip at the Annual Stallion Show at Newmarket.

A Royal Romance

Above left and right: Princess Anne with Peter and Zara at the Windsor Horse Trials.

Left: The Queen Mother and Prince Charles at the London premiere of *A Passage to India* at the Leicester Square Odeon.

Opposite above left: The Queen waves goodbye to the President of Mexico and his wife, who had just concluded a state visit in June 1985.

Opposite above right: At the beginning of 1986, speculation about a possible Royal engagement was mounting, and soon photographers were pursuing Sarah Ferguson. Here she is seen leaving her house in Clapham the morning before the engagement is made public.

Opposite below: Prince Andrew and Sarah Ferguson announced their engagement on March 19, 1986, with a summer wedding planned. They had met at a dinner party the previous year.

The Wedding of Andrew and Sarah

Left: Four months after their engagement, on July 23, 1986, Andrew and Sarah married at Westminster Abbey in a glittering ceremony conducted by the Archbishop of Canterbury, Dr. Robert Runcie. Prince Edward acted as best man. Ninety minutes before the service, the Queen conferred the title "Duke of York" on Prince Andrew, a title traditionally reserved for the sovereign's second son.

Below left: The newlyweds were at Ascot later in the year.

Below right: The Queen Mother and Prince Edward were among the congregation that attended a service at Hillington Parish Church near Sandringham.

Celebrations

Above left: Delighted family members congratulate Princess Anne after she wins the Dresden Diamond Stakes at Ascot races.

Above right: The Duke and Duchess of York with the Queen at the Royal Horse Trials.

Left: The Prince and Princess of Wales and the Queen join the Queen Mother to celebrate her 87th birthday. Here she greets well-wishers outside the gates of Clarence House.

The Birth of Princess Beatrice

Opposite above: A radiant Duchess of York and a beaming Duke introduced their first baby daughter to the world. Beatrice was born on August 8, 1988, at the Portland Hospital in London.

Opposite below right: Lord Snowdon and son Viscount Linley attend a society wedding.

Opposite below left: Earlier in the year, the Queen and Prince Philip attended the Maundy Service, at Lichfield Cathedral. During the service she distributed the Royal Maundy Money to 62 men and 62 women, all aged over 65 years and from the Diocese of Lichfield.

Above left: The Queen planting the "Chelsea Sentinel" on the grounds of the Royal Hospital, Chelsea.

Above right: Here Her Majesty is pictured with the Right Reverend Keith Sutton, Lord Bishop of Lichfield.

Left: The Queen greets young well-wishers on a traditional walkabout.

Trooping the Color

Top left: Members of the family were on the balcony to watch the Queen's birthday parade after the Trooping the Color ceremony in June 1988. (Left to right) Prince William, the Princess of Wales holding Prince Harry, Lady Rose Windsor, and Princess Michael with Lady Gabriella Windsor.

Middle left: Princess Diana was an incredibly active and popular member of the Royal Family. Here she greets the crowds as she visits St. Catherine's Hospice in Crawley, Surrey.

Left: Prince Harry and Prince William were captivated as they watched an 11-plane flyby after the Trooping the Color ceremony in 1989. It was the first time Prince Harry had taken part in the carriage procession.

Above: The Queen opened a conference at Westminster Hall.

The Birth of Princess Eugenie

Above left: The Duke and Duchess of York arriving at Heathrow Airport with Beatrice and new baby Eugenie (born on March 23, 1990) after flying back from Buenos Aires. They had been to Argentina to visit the Duchess's stepfather, Hector Barrantes, who had cancer.

Above center: Princess Diana arrives at the Canon Cinema, Shaftesbury Avenue, for the premiere of *LA Story*.

Above right: Princess Anne accompanied her mother to the "Joy to the World" concert at the Royal Albert Hall to mark the 70th anniversary of the Save the Children Fund. The Princess Royal has been President of this charity since 1970.

Left: The Queen surveys the Balmoral Estate while out riding. She had spent a great deal of time making Balmoral a viable commercial business.

William's School Days

Above middle: Prince William pictured during his final year at Wetherby School. Here he is attending the Harvest Festival at St. Matthew's Church, Bayswater, London.

Above right: He was soon playing soccer at Wetherby School and was selected to play in the first match of the season against Bassett House of Kensington.

Above left: William's final Sports Day at Wetherby School ended in tears, after he was disciplined by his mother for disobeying her.

Below left: William was met by headmaster Gerald Barber as he began his first day at boarding school in September 1990, attending Ludgrove School in Berkshire.

Opposite above: Diana was introduced to Elton John at the Aldwych Theatre, where she attended a fund-raising performance of *Tango Argentino*. The money collected was donated to the National Aids Trust.

Opposite below left: The Queen hands over the trophy to Australia at the Rugby Union World Cup in 1991.

Opposite below right: The Duchess of York flew back to London with her daughter Beatrice after a two-day trip to Disneyland with Pamela Stephenson and her three daughters. The following day Beatrice was due to start at Upton House School in Windsor.

Lady Helen Marries

Above left: Lady Helen Windsor married art dealer Tim Taylor at St. George's Chapel, Windsor, in July 1992.

Above right: Members of the Royal Family turned out for the wedding in force. Prince Charles and Prince Andrew lead, followed by Princess Anne and Prince Edward, with Diana behind in a vivid green outfit.

Right: The Duke of Edinburgh salutes over 1,000 servicemen and women who had served in the Gulf War. Crowds cheered as members of the armed forces marched through the City of London, with the Royal Family taking the official salute from the Mansion House.

Opposite above right: Continuing with her charity work, Diana attended a dinner at the Mansion House to mark the launch of the Re Action Trust, a charitable venture involving industry and Help the Aged.

Opposite below right: Members of the family leave church after the service on Christmas morning. Later that day in her speech to the nation, the Queen made it clear that she had no intention of abdicating, ending the speculation that she might step down on the 40th anniversary of her accession.

Opposite left: The Duchess of York leaves Upton House with her younger daughter Eugenie.

Princess Anne Remarries

Below right: Princess Anne married Commander Timothy Laurence, former Equerry to the Queen, at Crathie Church, near Balmoral. The wedding took place on December 12, 1992, with the couple determined to keep it a very private occasion. After the service, the newlyweds drove away in their Range Rover.

Above left: Sarah, Duchess of York, keeps a tight hand on Beatrice and Eugenie.

Above right: Prince William and Prince Harry with their great-grandmother and grandfather.

Opposite above and below left: Thorpe Park amusement park proved a firm favorite with Prince William and Prince Harry, who enjoyed a day there with their mother in 1993.

Opposite below right: William getting the hang of things on a skiing trip to Austria.

Meeting the Public

Opposite above: The Queen points a stern finger as she enjoys a day at Epsom races with her mother and son.

Opposite below left: The Duke of Edinburgh, with his three sons and grandson Peter Phillips, were among the members of the family who attended a carol service at the church near Sandringham.

Opposite below right: The Queen Mother at the Remembrance Service in Westminster Abbey, 1993.

Right: Princess Diana makes a visit to the Royal Hospital to meet the Chelsea Pensioners.

Below left: Later in the year at Bisley in Surrey, the Queen was given the opportunity to fire the last shot at the event using an SA80 rifle.

Below right: A chance for the Queen to go shopping at Windsor Horse Show.

93rd Birthday

Above: The family gather at Clarence House for the Queen Mother's 93rd birthday.

Left: Later that evening, the Queen Mother was at the Prince Edward Theatre with her daughter.

Opposite above: William arrives at Wimbledon to watch the Women's Singles final.

Opposite below left: William with his father.

Opposite below right: Harry looks happy as he leaves a shop with his mother.

William and Harry

Left: Already an accomplished rider, Harry took part in the Beaufort Hunt when he was 11.

Below left and right: Prince William and Prince Harry leave the Chicago Rib Shack in Knightsbridge, London, in January 1995.

Opposite above left: A St. Patrick's Day visit for the Queen Mother to the Irish Guards Barracks in London for the annual distribution of shamrocks.

Opposite above middle: The Queen enjoying the Windsor Horse Show in 1995.

Opposite above right: An eager grandmother arrives at the home of Daniel and Lady Sarah Chatto, who were awaiting the birth of their first child.

Opposite below left: The Queen and Queen Mother watch the 50th anniversary of the Victory in Europe celebrations in London from the balcony of Buckingham Palace.

Opposite below right: William started at Eton school in 1995. There he achieved both academic and sporting success. He gained nine GCSE and three A level certificates. He was a very good swimmer and a fearless soccer player, who was soon selected to play for the school team.

A Son for Lady Sarah

Left: Lady Sarah Chatto and her husband Daniel leave the Portland Hospital in London with their four-day-old son. He was later named Samuel David Benedict Chatto.

Below left and right: William with his parents and brother at Eton. Although by now the Prince and Princess were in the process of divorcing, the family arrived together.

Queen's 70th Birthday

Above left and right: The Queen chose to celebrate her 70th birthday with minimum fuss. After attending a church service at Sandringham with Princess Anne, she spent time afterward talking to children, many of whom presented her with flowers.

Below left: Camilla Parker Bowles with her son Tom and daughter Laura, at Henry Dent-Brocklehurst's 30th birthday party at the Café Royal. She was later seen chatting to her ex-husband Andrew and his new wife Rosemary.

Below right: Prince William and Peter and Zara Phillips share a joke as they leave church after the Christmas Day service at Sandringham.

William's Confirmation

Opposite far left: The family were united for Prince William's confirmation at St. George's Chapel in Windsor in March 1997. It was the first time Charles and Diana had appeared together in public since their divorce the previous August.

Opposite above right: On arrival in Fredericton, Canada, Prince Charles's first duty was to inspect the honor guard mounted by the 2nd Battalion, Royal Canadian Regiment.

Opposite below right: Prince Harry on vacation at Klosters. After many skiing trips he had become a confident and able skier.

Above: On a visit to Duku Duku in South Africa, Charles and Harry took time out to watch some Zulu dancing.

Right: The boys at Polvier by the Dee River in Scotland with their father. It was near the end of this summer vacation that they would hear the tragic news of their mother's death.

The Death of Princess Diana

Above: On August 30, 1997, Princess Diana was tragically killed in a high-speed car crash in Paris. Prince William and Prince Harry, who were with their father at Balmoral at the time, were informed the following morning. Immediately after the announcement was made public, a massive outpouring of grief seemed to sweep Britain, with floral tributes swamping the entrance to Kensington Palace.

Left: Prince Charles attempts to console his sons.

Opposite above: Diana's funeral took place at Westminster Abbey on September 6, 1997. One million people were estimated to have lined the procession route.

Opposite below: Charles, Prince Philip, Prince William, Prince Harry, and Earl Spencer, Diana's brother, stand in silence as the coffin is carried past them into the Abbey.

Clarence House

Opposite above: The family gathers at Clarence House to celebrate the Queen Mother's 98th birthday.

Opposite below: Prince William and Zara Phillips share a secret during the celebrations.

Right: The Queen, looking somber, is seen here at St. Mary's Cathedral, Kuala Lumpur. She had just learned of the death of Susan Barrantes, mother of the Duchess of York.

Below left: A reflective Zara Phillips.

Below right: The Queen Mother and Princess Margaret share a carriage to go to the Trooping the Color ceremony in 1998.

Edward and Sophie

Opposite above left and right: The Queen's youngest child, Edward, announced his engagement to Sophie Rhys-Jones in January 1999. The couple posed for photographs and walked on the grounds of St. James's Palace.

Right: Edward and his future wife, Sophie, looked happy as they watched the Queen's birthday salute on the balcony at Buckingham Palace, a week before their wedding.

Opposite below and Below: The couple were married on June 19, 1999, at St. George's Chapel, Windsor. After the ceremony they traveled back to the reception at Windsor Castle in a coach, waving to the crowds as they did so. Afterward, Edward was given the title Earl of Wessex and Sophie became Her Royal Highness the Countess of Wessex.

Outdoor Pursuits

Opposite above: Princess Anne and her daughter, Zara Phillips, riding on the grounds of Windsor Castle.

Opposite below: Prince William and Prince Harry joking with their father following William's first driving lesson at Highgrove in July 1999. His lesson had been given by police driving instructor Sergeant Chris Gilbert.

Above and left: Prince William and Prince Harry developed a closer relationship with their father in the years following the death of Princess Diana. Here they are pictured enjoying a skiing trip together at Klosters, Switzerland.

The Queen Mother's 100th Birthday

A host of notable Royal birthdays took place in 2000—Princess Margaret celebrated her 70th, the Princess Royal her 50th, Prince William turned 21, and the Duke of York was 40. However, it was the Queen Mother's 100th birthday that stood out as the landmark anniversary, and her whole family helped her celebrate.

Opposite above right: In July, the Royal Family attended a Thanksgiving Service at St. Paul's Cathedral to celebrate the Queen Mother's life. The Princess Royal, the Earl and Countess of Wessex, Prince Andrew, Peter Phillips, and Princess Beatrice and Princess Eugenie are seen standing on the steps after the service.

Right: Princess Eugenie and Princess Beatrice waved to the crowds as they left St. Paul's after the Thanksgiving Service.

Below: Members of the Royal Family joined the Queen Mother on the balcony of Buckingham Palace on her 100th birthday, August 4, 2000.

Opposite above left: Princess Beatrice with her father, the Duke of York, after they and the rest of the Royal Family attended a Sunday service at St. Mary Magdalene Church in Sandringham, Norfolk.

The Queen Mother Turns 101

Above: The Queen Mother walked out of Clarence House with the aid of her walking canes to greet the crowds on her 101st birthday. Accompanying her are: front row left to right, Princess Beatrice, Queen Elizabeth II, Princess Eugenie, and the Duke of York; back row left to right, the Duke of Edinburgh, Prince Harry, Prince Charles, Prince William, Zara Phillips, Peter Phillips, the Princess Royal, Lady Sarah Chatto, and Commander Tim Laurence.

Left: Prince Harry at the Six Nations Rugby Tournament.

Opposite above: Prince Harry with his cousin, Zara Phillips, at the Sandringham Christmas Service.

Opposite below: Prince William and Prince Harry after the Sandringham Service.

The Deaths of Princess Margaret and The Queen Mother

Opposite above: The Queen's Golden Jubilee celebrations, to mark 50 years as monarch, were set to dominate the Royal year, but this was not to be. After suffering heart problems following a stroke, the Queen's sister, Princess Margaret, died on February 9, 2002, at the age of 71. Less than two months later, in her 102nd year, the Queen Mother died peacefully in her sleep at Windsor. Here the Earl and Countess of Wessex view the flowers left by members of the public for the Queen Mother.

Opposite below: The Queen Mother lay in state for five days in Westminster Hall, where mourners filed past the coffin to pay their respects.

Above left: Princes William and Harry following the gun carriage that carried the Queen Mother's coffin to Westminster Hall for her lying-in-state.

Above middle: The funeral took place on April 9, 2002, at Westminster Abbey. Here Prince Charles, visibly moved, watches the coffin leaving the Abbey.

Above right: The Queen arriving at Westminster Abbey for a memorial service for Princess Margaret.

Left: The Queen out riding on the grounds of Windsor Castle.

The Golden Jubilee

Opposite above left: In June 2002, Queen Elizabeth II celebrated her Golden Jubilee, having reigned for 50 years. The event was marked by extensive celebrations, including a thanksgiving service at St. Paul's Cathedral, a parade and carnival along The Mall, a flyby, the Party at the Palace concert (at Buckingham Palace), and a huge fireworks display. Here the Queen makes her way to St. Paul's in the gold state coach, which she had previously used only for her coronation and Silver Jubilee celebrations.

Opposite above right: Edward and Sophie, the Earl and Countess of Wessex, leave Buckingham Palace for St. Paul's in an open-top coach.

Opposite below: The Duke of York, Prince Harry, and Prince William arriving at St. Paul's.

Left: Andrew, the Duke of York, and Prince William also ride in an open carriage as part of the procession, accompanied by a mounted escort.

Below: Prince William, Prince Charles, and the Queen sharing a joke as they observe the spectacular carnival in The Mall.

Renewing her Vows

Opposite: Another milestone was reached with the 50th anniversary of the Queen's Coronation on June 2, 2003. A service at Westminster Abbey on the day, saw the Queen renewing her vows of 50 years ago. Here the Queen and the Duke of Edinburgh are led in procession by the Dean of Westminster, the Very Reverend Dr. Wesley Carr, at the start of the service in Westminster Abbey.

Above: The Queen and Prince Philip with their grandsons Prince William and Prince Harry on the balcony after the Trooping the Color.

Left: The Queen and Prince Philip visiting St. Bartholomew the Great Church in the City of London.

President Bush

Opposite above: President George W. Bush and Mrs. Bush met the Queen and Prince Philip at Buckingham Palace on their first state visit to Britain in November 2003.

Opposite below left: Prince Charles with former glider pilots at the Pegasus Bridge Monument in Normandy on the anniversary of D-Day in June 2004.

Opposite below right: In July 2004, Prince Charles visited the site of a more recent conflict, the Old Bridge in Mostar, Bosnia, which had recently been rebuilt.

Left: July 2004 also saw the Party in the Park at London's Hyde Park, in aid of the Prince's Trust. Prince Charles is pictured with the singer Jamelia, who is an ambassador for the organization.

Below: The Diana Memorial Fountain was officially opened in Hyde Park during the summer of 2004. Prince Charles and his sons attended the unveiling by the Queen on July 6.

The Wedding of Charles and Camilla

Opposite above left: More than 30 years after they first met, the Prince of Wales and Camilla Parker Bowles were married in a civil ceremony at Windsor Guildhall on April 9, 2004. This was followed by a blessing by the Archbishop of Canterbury in St. George's Chapel and then a reception for 800 guests in the state apartments at Windsor Castle. Here guests and spectators arrive for the wedding in Windsor.

Left and Opposite above right: Prince Charles and his new bride, now known as the Duchess of Cornwall, left St. George's Chapel after the blessing to a warm reception from the waiting crowds.

Below: The Duchess of Cornwall at St. George's Chapel.

Opposite below: Members of the Royal Family gather around the Royal couple after the blessing at St. George's Chapel.

A Family Affair

Opposite above: The newly married couple at Windsor.

Opposite below: Prince Harry, Zara Phillips, and Prince William at the wedding.

Above: Prince William, Prince Harry, and Peter and Zara Phillips pictured following the marriage blessing at St. George's Chapel.

Far left: Prince William arriving at the Guildhall in Windsor.

Left: Prince Charles and the Duchess of Cornwall leave the Guildhall after their civil ceremony, followed by Princes William and Harry.

William Graduates

Right: In June 2005, Prince William graduated from the University of St. Andrews, having gained a Master's degree in Geography.

Below: In the same month, the Prince and the Duchess arrived in the royal carriage for Ladies' Day at the Royal Ascot horse race. The event was held at York because of construction work being undertaken at Ascot Racecourse.

Opposite left: The Duchess of Cornwall is pictured with Prince Charles opening a playground near Balmoral, her first official engagement since her marriage.

Opposite above right: In October 2005, on a state visit to Lithuania, the Queen attended a banquet at the Presidential Palace hosted by President Valdas Adamkus.

Opposite below right: The Queen while on a visit to a dairy farm in Clitheroe, Lancashire, in May 2006.

The Queen at 80

Left: The Queen turned 80 on April 21, 2006, and many celebrations and events took place both around this date and on her official birthday on June 17. Services of thanksgiving were held, along with lunches, dinners, fireworks displays, receptions, and even a children's party at Buckingham Palace. Here the family gather on the steps of St. Paul's Cathedral after the thanksgiving service (left to right): the Earl and Countess of Wessex, Prince Charles, Prince Harry, Prince William, Princess Beatrice, and the Duke of York. The Princess Royal and Commander Tim Laurence can be seen in the background.

Below: The Queen and the Duke of Edinburgh in full regalia attending the Order of the Garter Ceremony at Windsor Castle.

The Family Celebrates

Above right: To celebrate her 80th birthday, the Queen took her family on a cruise around the Western Isles of Scotland in July on the *Hebridean Princess*. Princesses Beatrice and Eugenie are pictured on their way to the boat.

Above left: Prince Charles pictured aboard the cruise liner.

Left: Viscount and Viscountess Linley and the Honorable Margarita Armstrong-Jones along with Lady Sarah Chatto and Daniel Chatto.

Opposite above left: Princess Anne and her husband Tim Laurence board the ship.

Opposite above right: Celebrations continued as the Queen toured Lithuania.

Opposite below: Prince William, on parade at Sandhurst in December 2006, struggles to hide his amusement as the Queen, his grandmother, inspects the troops.

Willam Meets Kate

Left: Prince William and his girlfriend Catherine (Kate) Middleton on the slopes in the Swiss resort of Zermatt in March 2007. They met at St. Andrews University while he was studying geography and Kate majored in the history of art. She soon became the center of much media attention as their relationship deepened and speculation about their future together began to grow.

Far left: The Queen leaving Westminster Abbey after attending the annual Commonwealth Day Observance.

Below: Private Kevin Challis is presented with his Iraq medal by the Queen at Howe Barracks in Canterbury. He had received major injuries to his arm and back during an Iraqi ambush.

Zara Phillips MBE

Left: Zara Phillips was awarded an MBE by her grandmother the Queen in November 2007, for services to equestrianism. She had won the BBC Sports Personality of the Year the previous December, along with a gold medal at the World Equestrian Games.

Top: (left to right) Princess Anne, Vice Admiral Timothy Laurence, Zara Phillips, and Mike Tindall outside Buckingham Palace after the ceremony.

Above: Zara Phillips pictured during the European Eventing Championship in 2007, when the British team took the gold medal.

The Queen's Diamond Wedding Anniversary

Opposite above: Prince William and Prince Harry arriving at Westminster Abbey with Prince Charles and Camilla, Duchess of Cornwall, for a service to celebrate the 60th wedding anniversary of the Queen and Prince Philip.

Opposite below left, middle, and right: Prince Andrew (left), the Countess of Wessex with Prince Philip (middle), and Princess Anne (right) walk to St. George's Chapel, Windsor, for the Easter Sunday Service.

Right: A happy, smiling Queen celebrates her 60th wedding anniversary.

Below: Princesses Beatrice and Eugenie with the Duchess of Cornwall and Prince Charles at Royal Ascot races in June 2008.

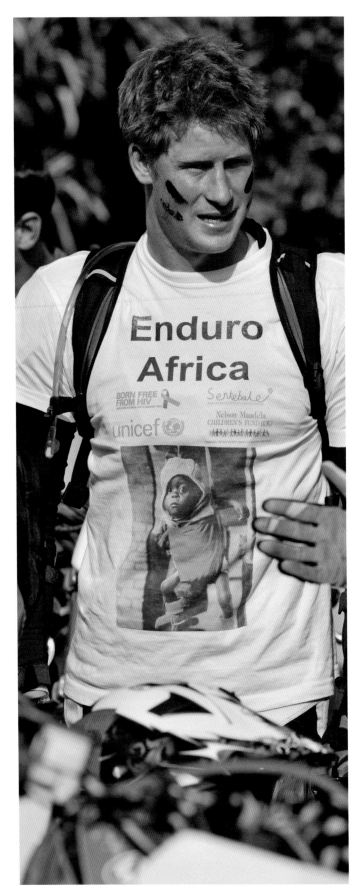

The Princes In South Africa

Opposite: Prince William and Prince Harry at the start of the 1,000-mile, eight-day Enduro Africa motorcycle ride across South Africa. They were racing with 80 other competitors from Durban to Port Elizabeth to raise funds for Unicef, the Nelson Mandela Children's Fund, and Sentebale. Prince Harry set up the Sentebale charity in 2006 with Prince Seeiso of Lesotho, with much of their work supporting children in Lesotho orphaned through HIV and AIDS.

Above and right: During the ride, the brothers played in a soccer match against a local team from the remote village of Igxarho in Morgan's Bay on the Eastern Cape.

Tribute To The Queen Mother

Opposite above: A statue of Queen Elizabeth, the Queen Mother, was unveiled by Queen Elizabeth II in London in February 2009. The 9-foot-high memorial depicts the Queen Mother wearing Order of the Garter robes and is positioned in front of the statue of her late husband King George VI. It is flanked by two bronze reliefs showing the Queen Mother visiting families made homeless by bombs during World War II and enjoying the races at Ascot. Standing in front of the memorial are (left to right) the Duke of Edinburgh, the Queen, the Duchess of Cornwall, and the Prince of Wales.

Opposite below left: Princess Beatrice and Princess Eugenie at the unveiling ceremony.

Opposite below right: Zara Phillips arrives at Cheltenham racecourse in March 2009.

Above: The Queen watches her horse, Barbers Shop, during the Gold Cup at the Cheltenham Festival of Racing.

Right: Prince Charles speaking at a conference organized by his personal charity, the Prince's Foundation for the Built Environment. Addressing an international audience at St. James's Palace, he spoke about the "brutal and insensitive process of globalization" and centered on the need to respect the indigenous cultures and traditions, allowing people to keep their sense of community when developing an increasingly globalized world.

Ascot Races

The Queen and Prince Philip (left) along with Prince Charles and the Duchess of Cornwall (above) arrive in traditional carriages for the second day at Royal Ascot in June 2009.

Opposite: Prince Harry competes in the Dorchester Trophy charity polo match at Cirencester Park polo club.

Celebrating Peace

Left: The Queen and Prince Philip leave the Service of Commemoration, held at St. Paul's Cathedral, to mark the end of the hostilities with Iraq.

Below left: The service, held in October 2009, was also attended by the Prince of Wales and the Duchess of Cornwall, accompanied by Prince William.

Below right: The Prince of Wales, colonel-in-chief of the Mercian Regiment, presents Private Dean Housley from the 2nd Battalion of the Mercian Regiment with a medal for service in Afghanistan, where he had been injured by a mine on his first tour.

Opposite above left: Prince William chats to young children from the hospital nursery at the Alder Hey Children's Hospital, Liverpool.

Opposite above right: Prince Charles with veterans at the annual parade and service of the Combined Cavalry Old Comrades Association.

Opposite below left: In a moment of father-son merriment, Prince Harry, referred to as Lieutenant Henry Wales, received his provisional wings from his father.

Opposite below right: Queen Elizabeth II with Jacob Zuma, the President of South Africa, during a state banquet at Buckingham Palace.

Battle Of Britain Service

Right: The Duchess of Cornwall and Prince William arrive at Westminster Abbey for the Battle of Britain service of Thanksgiving and Rededication.

Below left and right: Somber moments for the family during the service.

Opposite above left: The Duchess of Cornwall meets families of the injured patients during a visit to the New Queen Elizabeth Hospital and The Royal Centre for Defence Medicine in Birmingham.

Opposite above right: The Prince of Wales took the opportunity to meet the military and civilian medical staff at the hospital.

Opposite below: Prince Charles and the Duchess of Cornwall joke with the stallholders as they tour Brixton Market, London, in July 2010.

William and Kate Engaged

Above and left: Clarence House announced Prince William and Kate Middleton's engagement on November 16, 2010. It was revealed that the couple had become engaged during a visit to Kenya the previous month. William gave her the sapphire and diamond engagement ring that had belonged to his mother.

Opposite above left: Kate Middleton carried out her first formal engagement in February 2011, when she and Prince William launched a new Atlantic 85 inshore lifeboat at Trearddur Bay Lifeboat Station in Anglesey.

Opposite above right: Taking on her new role with ease, Kate chats happily to the waiting children at the lifeboat station.

Opposite below left and right: Waving to the crowds which had gathered for the occasion, Kate impressed locals with her grasp of the Welsh language. The couple were living in a rented home on Anglesey while Prince William was working as a search and rescue pilot.

The Wedding of William and Kate

Above: William and Kate's wedding took place on April 29, 2011. An estimated 2 billion people around the world watched as Kate's father, Michael, escorted his daughter from the Goring Hotel into a Rolls-Royce Phantom VI for their journey to Westminster Abbey. The bride carried a delicate bouquet filled with myrtle, lily of the valley, hyacinth, and Sweet William. Kate had chosen her sister Pippa as maid-of-honor while William elected to have his brother Harry as his best man.

Above right: Kate's dress, a closely guarded secret before the wedding day, was designed by Sarah Burton at Alexander McQueen. Made of satin, it featured a lace appliqué bodice made at the Royal School of Needlework at Hampton Court Palace. The train measured nearly 9 feet, and she wore a Cartier tiara lent to her by the Queen.

Below right: As the bridal procession began the three-and-a-half-minute walk down the aisle, they were watched by 1,900 invited guests while the choir sang an anthem by Sir Hubert Parry. The wedding service was led by The Dean of Westminster, John Hall, assisted by Rowan Williams, Archbishop of Canterbury, and Richard Chartres, the Bishop of London.

Opposite: As the wedding bells pealed, the newly married couple emerged in front of the waiting crowds. William had chosen to wear the full dress uniform of the Irish Guards with the blue sash that he was entitled to wear as a Knight of the Order of the Garter. Immediately after the ceremony, the Queen bestowed the title of Duke and Duchess of Cambridge on the couple.

Homeward Bound

Opposite above: The Prince of Wales and the Duchess of Cornwall travel back to Buckingham Palace after the ceremony with Michael and Carole Middleton.

Opposite below left: Kate and William made their journey through the streets of London in a 1902 state landau drawn by four white horses. Her wedding ring had been made from Welsh gold, a Royal Family tradition since 1923.

Opposite below right: A dazzling smile from Pippa Middleton.

Above: Prince Harry escorts Lady Louise Windsor back to the palace.

The World Looks On

Right: Princess Eugenie of York (left), in Vivienne Westwood, and Princess Beatrice of York (right) in Valentino haute couture arrive at Westminster Abbey for the wedding.

Above: Cousin Zara Phillips, soon to be married herself, makes her way to the ceremony.

Just Married

Above: Time for the now-traditional kiss on the balcony as Margarita Armstrong-Jones (right) and Grace van Cutsem watch.

Right: After the lunchtime reception Prince William drove his bride back to Clarence House in his father's Aston Martin. Decorated by Prince Harry, the registration number read "JU5T WED." A private reception, hosted by the Prince of Wales, followed that evening.

Overleaf: During the lunchtime reception, hosted by the Queen, the wedding party made their traditional appearance on the balcony of Buckingham Palace. The celebrations included a flyby from the Battle of Britain Memorial Flight, with a Lancaster flanked by a Hurricane and a Spitfire.

Newlyweds

Opposite: After their honeymoon on a private island in the Seychelles, the Duke and Duchess were at Epsom Downs to watch Mickael Barzalona win the Derby on Pour Moi.

Above left: Prince William and Prince Harry leave the field after competing against each other in the Sentebale Royal Salute Polo Cup, held at Coworth Park in Berkshire. Prince William's team won the trophy, and the fundraising event for Prince Harry's charity continued into the evening with dinner, dancing, and an auction.

Above right and Right: Prince William competing in a polo match at Chester racecourse.

The Duke of Edinburgh's 90th Birthday

Opposite above left: Beaming bride-to-be Zara Phillips arrives at St. George's Chapel, Windsor, to join the celebrations for the Duke of Edinburgh's 90th birthday on June 12, 2011. Seven hundred and fifty guests joined the Duke for the church service led by the Dean of Windsor and afterward attended a reception held at St. George's Hall in Windsor Castle.

Opposite below: The following week Prime Minister David Cameron and his wife Samantha invited the Queen and the Duke of Edinburgh to Downing Street for a celebratory birthday lunch.

Opposite above right: David Beckham and Zara Phillips launch the Samsung Olympic Torch Relay nomination campaign. The Olympic 2012 committee had invited the public to nominate any "unsung heroes" living in the United Kingdom to carry the Olympic torch for part of its journey to the stadium. A total of 8,000 people were to be selected.

Left and below: The Duke and Duchess of Cambridge pictured at Wimbledon in 2011.

Capturing
North American Hearts

Above: At the end of June 2011, William and Kate set off on their first official overseas tour. With the eyes of the world following them, they completed a highly successful 11-day visit to the United States and Canada. Halfway into the itinerary, they spent two days in Calgary where they were greeted by Prime Minister Stephen Harper and presented with white Smithbilt cowboy hats. A rodeo demonstration at the BMO Center was followed by a visit to the Calgary Stampede the following day.

Left: The couple then flew on to Los Angeles where they attended a private reception at the British Consul-General's residence. Crowds gathered throughout the tour with the Canadian and American people eager to meet Prince William and his bride.

Zara Phillips Marries

Left and below right: Zara Phillips married English rugby star Mike Tindall on July 30, 2011. The couple chose to have a private ceremony, held at the Canongate Kirk in Edinburgh, followed by a reception in the Palace of Holyroodhouse. Crowds gathered in force along the Royal Mile to watch members of the Royal Family arrive for their second wedding of the year.

Below left: Prince Harry, Prince William, and the Duchess of Cambridge were among the guests.

The wedding was one of many happy and successful occasions for the Royal Family in 2011. The festivities continued throughout 2012 as the country celebrated the 60th anniversary of the Queen's accession to the throne and enjoyed the events planned to mark her Diamond Jubilee.

Posted to the Falkland Islands

Above left: After spending Christmas with his wife, Prince William left to serve in the Falkland Islands. He joined the Search and Rescue Squadron at RAF Mount Pleasant for a six-week deployment, part of a four-man crew providing cover for both the civilian and military population.

Above right: A royal visit to Greenland Pier to see the 94-foot row barge that had been built to lead the Thames River Diamond Jubilee Pageant. The vessel was the first royal barge to be built in 100 years, and the Queen named her "Gloriana." The design was inspired by Canaletto's famous 18th century painting of a Thames pageant and incorporates sweet chestnut wood taken from Prince Charles's Duchy of Cornwall estate.

Left: The Queen and the Duchesses pose outside Fortnum & Mason in London. Inside, the Queen showed great interest in the display of Diamond Jubilee products, especially the tea and cookies, which were being sent to members of the armed forces to mark her 60 years on the throne.

Opposite: Although the main Diamond Jubilee celebrations took place over June 2–5, the Jubilee was also marked by the Queen making official visits to major cities across the whole of Britain. Other senior members of the Royal Family made visits on her behalf to every Realm, Commonwealth country, Crown Dependency, and British Overseas Territory.

The Queen's Diamond Jubilee

Opposite above and Left:
Even driving rain failed to spoil the Thames Jubilee Pageant on June 3, 2012, to mark the 60th anniversary of the accession of Queen Elizabeth II. The royal row barge *Gloriana*—powered by Olympic gold medalists Sir Matthew Pinsent and Sir Steve Redgrave, rowing with 16 others —led a flotilla of 1,000 boats down the Thames River from Albert Bridge to Tower Bridge. At the heart of the flotilla, aboard the river cruiser *Spirit of Chartwell*, the Queen and the Duke of Edinburgh braved the elements for more than an hour to wave to the crowds who gathered along the route to celebrate.

One Million People Gather

Opposite below left: The Duke of Edinburgh and Princes William and Harry appeared in military dress uniforms in honor of the occasion. An estimated 1 million people had gathered on the banks of the Thames to cheer as the flotilla—including shallops, steamers, Dunkirk little ships, tugs, cruisers, kayaks, dragon boats, river cruisers, and many more—went past.

Opposite below right: The Duchess of Cornwall and the Duchess of Cambridge were also on board the *Spirit of Chartwell*, which was decorated with 10,000 flowers from the royal estates.

Right: Prince Charles greets his mother. The stunning gold dress the Queen wore at the Diamond Jubilee concert was created from fabric bought on an overseas tour in 1961, which had been stored in tissue paper until she found a use for it.

A Weekend of Celebration

Right and Far right: As part of the Jubilee celebrations, the Queen attended a service of thanksgiving at St. Paul's Cathedral without the Duke of Edinburgh, who had been taken to the hospital as a precaution after coming down with an infection.

Below: Despite having to appear without her husband—who she had described as being "my strength and my stay all these years"—the Queen still managed to look delighted and cheerful as she waved to crowds from the balcony at Buckingham Palace with Prince William, the Duchess of Cambridge, and Prince Harry. Thousands of well-wishers had waited for hours in the rain, and they cheered and applauded throughout the royal party's appearance on the balcony.

An Historic Visit

Left: Thousands looked on as the Queen and Prince Philip were driven around the Stormont estate in Belfast in an open-top vehicle on June 27, 2012. The visit to Northern Ireland was part of the Jubilee tour around Britain, but became even more significant when the Queen shook hands with Northern Ireland's Deputy First Minister and former IRA commander Martin McGuinness for the first time—a milestone in Anglo-Irish relations.

Below right: The Queen waves as she leaves the Anglican Cathedral in Enniskillen and crosses the road to St. Michael's Roman Catholic church, the first time in her 60-year reign that she had set foot in a Catholic church in Northern Ireland.

Below left: The Jubilee celebrations would not have been complete without a horse racing event—the Queen and the Duke of Edinburgh attend the 2012 Derby.

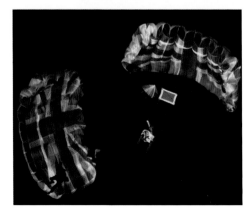

London 2012 Olympics

Above: Olympic torch bearer Gina MacGregor meets the Queen and Sebastian Coe on the grounds of Windsor Castle on Day 53 of the London Olympic 2012 Torch Relay.

Far left: Jacques Rogge, the President of the International Olympic Committee, speaking at a reception held by the Queen for members of the IOC at Buckingham Palace.

Left and Below left: The Queen was delighted with the short film shown during the London 2012 Olympic Games Opening Ceremony in which she was escorted from the palace by James Bond (actor Daniel Craig) before apparently parachuting into the stadium. The film had been made in secret in March, and even senior members of the Royal Family were taken completely by surprise.

Supporting Team GB

Above: The Duke and Duchess of Cambridge and Prince Harry cheer on the British Olympic team at the Velodrome on August 2. In the excitement of the moment, the Duke and Duchess later embraced each other in delight after the British team, Philip Hindes, Jason Kenny, and Sir Chris Hoy, won the Gold and set a new world record in the Men's Team Sprint Track Cycling final.

Left: Prince Harry is given a mascot by 14-year-old Australian Paralympic athlete Maddison Elliot. The prince was at the aquatics center on September 4 to cheer on Team GB in the London 2012 Paralympic Games; an avid sports fan he, William, and Kate were ambassadors for Team GB and managed to attend dozens of Olympic events.

A Royal Medal

Above: Zara Phillips rode High Kingdom in the Dressage Equestrian event on Day 2 of the Olympic Games, at Greenwich Park. Team GB won Silver in the event and their medals were presented by Princess Anne—who carefully placed one around her daughter's neck and then kissed her on both cheeks.

Left: The Princess Royal and Sir Clive Woodward watch Great Britain play France during a Paralympic Wheelchair Rugby match. Princess Anne is President of the British Olympic Association and a UK member of the International Olympic Committee. She was also a Board Member of the London Organizing Committee of the Olympic Games.

Visiting the Far East

Left: Kate and William admire the newly created orchid "Vanda William Catherine" during a visit to Singapore Botanical Gardens on September 11, 2012. The visit to Singapore was the first stop on the royal couple's Diamond Jubilee tour on behalf of the Queen.

Below: The royal couple enjoy a display of traditional dance during their visit to Guadalcanal Island on Day 7 of their Diamond Jubilee tour. The tour also took in Malaysia, Borneo, the Solomon Islands, and the tiny island of Tuvalu. The couple continued to appear happy and relaxed during their public appearances, although a French magazine had recently published topless photographs of Kate snatched during a private trip to the South of France, and the invasion of privacy had upset them deeply.

Expecting a Happy Event

Opposite above right: The Duchess is all smiles as she arrives at the National Portrait Gallery in April 2013. The previous December, news had broken that she and William were expecting their first child after she was admitted to the hospital with severe morning sickness.

Opposite above left: Prince Harry races to scramble his Apache helicopter at Camp Bastion. The Prince's tour in Afghanistan ended in January 2013.

Opposite below: After being shown a few "spell techniques," Kate and William took part in a "wand duel" on the set used to depict Diagon Alley in the Harry Potter movies, during the inauguration of Warner Bros. Studios at Leavesden, near London.

Above: Kate chats to participants at the National Review of Queen's Scouts at Windsor Castle.

Right: May 8, 2013: The Queen looks thoughtful as she travels in a horse-drawn carriage from Buckingham Palace to attend the State Opening of Parliament, where she will make a speech in the House of Lords to Members of Parliament and Peers which sets out the government's forthcoming legislative program.

Warrior Games

Above: Prince Harry hits the ball toward former US Olympic beach volleyball great Misty May-Treanor during an exhibition match of sitting volleyball at the Warrior Games, which were held at the US Olympic Training Center in Colorado Springs. Harry joined Team GB in the second set and helped to achieve victory over the US team. The Warrior Games, specifically for injured military personnel, were being held for the first time and Prince Harry later said he would like to bring the event to the UK.

Left: Prince Charles, Camilla, the Duchess of Cornwall, and the Duchess of Cambridge attend the first Garden Party of the summer on the grounds of Buckingham Palace on May 22, 2013. The Duchess of Cambridge, who was now over seven months pregnant, had not been expected to appear but told guests that the cooler weather had made her feel much more comfortable.

A Royal Garden Party

Above: The Queen speaks to members of the RAF Abingdon Volunteer Gliding Squadron during the second Garden Party, on May 30, 2013. Approximately 8,000 guests attend each party—people from all walks of life—and presentations are made at random as members of the royal party walk among the guests.

Right: The Queen and Prince Philip pictured during Derby Day, June 1, 2013. The event had come under threat when a brief power outage caused the elevators and the scales in the jockeys' Weighing Room to stop working—and the Queen was forced to forgo her traditional visit to the paddock because officials were afraid the royal party might become stuck in the elevator.

Celebrating the Coronation

Opposite: June 2013 marked the 60th anniversary of the coronation of Queen Elizabeth II—which had been held on June 2, 1953—and the anniversary was marked by a service at Westminster Abbey on June 4. Some of those who took part in the 1953 service were among the congregation, and the heavy, solid gold St. Edward's Crown was displayed on the High Altar—the first time it had left the Tower of London since 1953.

Left: Queen Elizabeth, seen here talking with the Dean of Westminster, John Hall, entered Westminster Abbey to the same music that had greeted her in 1953.

Below: Members of the Royal Family gathered outside Westminster Abbey after attending the service—including Prince William, the Duchess of Cambridge, Zara Phillips, who later announced that she was expecting a baby in 2014, Prince Harry, Peter Phillips, and Princess Eugenie.

A Royal Win at Ascot

Above: The Queen and her race advisor John Warren looked delighted as her horse Estimate won the famous Gold Cup race at Ascot on June 20, 2013. Although her horses had won races at Ascot in the past, the Gold Cup itself had always eluded her—and this was also the first time in the race's 207-year history that it had been won by a reigning monarch.

Top and right: The Queen traditionally presents the Gold Cup to the winning owner, but new arrangements were quickly made and she received the trophy from her son, the Duke of York.

A New Arrival

Top left and above: On July 22, 2013, the Duchess of Cambridge was taken to St. Mary's Hospital in London accompanied by Prince William, and during the day crowds gathered outside Buckingham Palace to wait for news. The Duchess gave birth to a son at 4:24 pm, but the traditional proclamation, displayed on an easel in the forecourt of the palace, did not appear until four hours later.

Top right: Prince Charles and the Duchess of Cornwall arrive at the hospital to meet the new prince the day after his birth.

Left: Carole and Michael Middleton told reporters that their new grandchild was "absolutely beautiful."

And Baby Makes Three

Above and opposite: Early in the evening of July 23, Kate and William appeared outside the hospital to show their baby for the first time to crowds of reporters, photographers, and well-wishers. William said they were "still working on a name" and that the baby "had a good pair of lungs on him." A short time later the new family left the hospital, with the young prince safely strapped into a car seat, to spend their first night together at Kensington Palace.

The Queen visited her newest great-grandchild at Kensington Palace on July 24—the first time that that a reigning monarch was able to meet a great-grandchild in direct line of succession since Queen Victoria met the future King Edward VIII in 1894. After the Queen's visit, it was announced that William and Kate's baby would be called Prince George Alexander Louis of Cambridge. He is third in line to the throne, after Prince Charles and Prince William, so the future of the Royal Family through the twenty-first century seems assured.

Acknowledgments

The photographs in this book are from the archives of the *Daily Mail*.

Particular thanks to Steve Torrington, Alan Pinnock,
Dave Sheppard, and Brian Jackson

Design by John Dunne.